MIRACLE MOMENTS IN
NEW YORK GIANTS
FOOTBALL HISTORY

Best Plays, Games, and Records

TOM ROCK

SPORTS PUBLISHING

Sports Publishing books may be purchased in bulk at special discounts for sales promotion, corporate gifts, fund-raising, or educational purposes. Special editions can also be created to specifications. For details, contact the Special Sales Department, Sports Publishing, 307 West 36th Street, 11th Floor, New York, NY 10018 or sportspubbooks@skyhorsepublishing.com.

Sports Publishing® is a registered trademark of Skyhorse Publishing, Inc.®, a Delaware corporation.

Visit our website at www.sportspubbooks.com.

10 9 8 7 6 5 4 3 2 1

Library of Congress Cataloging-in-Publication Data is available on file.

Photos on pages 26, 54, 68, 71, 87, 94, 96, 126, 133 Copyright © New York Football Giants, Inc. used with the permission of the copyright owner.

Cover design by Tom Lau
Cover photo credit Getty Images

ISBN: 978-1-68358-294-6
Ebook ISBN: 978-1-68358-295-3

Printed in China

For Giants fans near and far, past and future.

CONTENTS

The image caption reads, vertically: Al Bello / Staff, courtesy of Getty Images

Giants owner Wellington Mara presided over the team through some of the franchise's bleakest times, but he also saw them achieve glory in two Super Bowls.
(Newsday LLC/Kathy Kmonicek)

INTRODUCTION

It was a crisp fall day, one perfect for the playing or watching of football—the kind of day Wellington Mara would have loved to spend walking laps around the practice field while his boys put the finishing touches on the game plan to beat that week's opponent.

Only this crowd wasn't there to see a sporting event. They were there to mourn Wellington Mara.

The Giants' owner, the son of the team's founder and the inaugural squad's first ball boy, had died at age 89. St. Patrick's Cathedral in Manhattan was packed with those who came to remember him on October 28, 2005.

Edward Cardinal Egan conducted the mass. John Mara, Wellington's oldest son, delivered the eulogy. The pews were filled with a who's who of luminaries, not just from sport, but from New York society. Tiki Barber, one of Wellington's favorite players, had led the 2005–06 team into the church. He looked around the cavernous building, looked at the Hall of Famers and owners, the past and present commissioners who had assembled, looked at the regality of the event.

"It was unbelievable," Tiki told me. "Anybody who was anybody was there. And that place is so magical and massive and ornate and beautiful. You kind of forget sometimes how big the Giants are, how important and meaningful they are to the city of New York. That was a reminder of the impact that the Giants have had on the city over the history of their existence."

It is easy to forget. We follow the Giants' exploits on a daily basis. Back page to back page, victory to defeat, defeat to victory, embarrassment to ecstasy and back again. It's been that way for nearly a century, and it tends to blend together into a Big Blue blur.

But there are moments—like the one in St. Patrick's Cathedral for Tiki Barber—when the enormity of the Giants becomes clear. When they rise from the cacophony of noise that the city creates and remind everyone just how special the franchise is, the unique relationship it has with the area and its fans across the country and around the world. These are the Miracle Moments.

I've tried to keep that quote from Tiki in mind while I worked on this book, which attempts to collect as many of those moments as possible and present them in a package that spans the history of the organization.

Some of them were easy to pick out. There are games that were decided by sneakers, games in which an aging quarterback threw seven touchdown passes, games in which iconic players were knocked cold and retired from the sport only to come back, and games where it felt like the whole region was salsa dancing. There were draft-day decisions that yielded titles, backroom conversations that brought in or replaced head coaches and general managers, and there was a $500 investment that started it all.

This book has been sourced via a diverse array of channels. I spoke with dozens of former players, coaches, and executives. I poured over newspaper and magazine articles that have been published over the decades and touched base with some of the men and women who wrote them and were witnesses to history. I watched numerous television interviews and documentaries, listened back to classic radio calls on a few of the most significant games in NFL history.

There are some chapters where I can tell you firsthand about what happened. Since I was immersed in the team's locker room and on its sideline since 2008 covering the Giants for *Newsday*, much of the information on more recent events comes from details I reported personally at the time they took place. There are other chapters where all the major characters are long deceased and I've relied on previously published accounts to give them their voices. And then there are chapters like the one on Y.A. Tittle's seven-touchdown game against the Redskins where I spoke with Joe Walton, the tight end who caught three of those passes including the final one, and I basically got the heck out of the way to let him tell the story.

Throughout the course of reporting for this book, I would often ask sources what they thought was the biggest Miracle Moment in Giants history. Most pointed to championships. Many said that David Tyree's helmet catch would never be topped. "That," Carl Banks told me as succinctly as possible, "that's *the* moment."

But others had more personal recollections. Things like studying the winds at Giants Stadium for a strategic advantage, seeing a lone captain walk to midfield in a Super Bowl like the marshal from an old western movie.

There are, undoubtedly, Miracle Moments that didn't make the cut here. And that's okay. Miracles don't have to be enjoyed by everyone to prove their worth. Sometimes they happen in private and are more special because of the fewer people who know about them. Personal miracles. You may remember watching the ball go wide right while sitting on your grandfather's knee or retweeting the video clip of the craziest one-handed catch anyone had ever seen. You may remember visiting a cemetery to share the news of a big win or making a trip as a kid to watch a training camp practice and gawk at the in-person immensity of the men who looked so small on the television screen. Maybe you recall the first time you bundled up and walked into Yankee Stadium to see a football game, the first time you made your way up the spiral ramp at Giants Stadium, or, God help you, the first time you sat in the Yale Bowl to watch the worst team in the NFL.

When I asked John Mara for his Miracle Moment, he, like more than a few others, said it would be hard to top winning Super Bowl XLII, a game against the previously unbeaten Patriots in which no one gave the Giants a chance to even compete. But then, after a quick pause, he was able to.

It was the last game of the 1981 season. The Giants beat the Cowboys at Giants Stadium, and they still needed the Jets to win the following day to make the playoffs for the first time since 1963 (which they did). Somehow, that wasn't as important as the feeling that for the first time in 17 years, they were pointed in the right direction.

After the game, the elevators from the press box level where he and his father had watched were broken, so the two of them had to walk down one of those winding spiral ramps that stood in each corner of the building. This was just three years after The Fumble against the Eagles, three years after people were burning tickets and flying banners and hanging Wellington Mara in effigy from the upper deck. Now he was among the fans who had voiced that dissatisfaction so loudly and so clearly.

"To walk down with him, to have people congratulating him and slapping him on the back and all that stuff, that to me is a moment that probably compares with any of the Super Bowl wins," John Mara said.

You want a personal Miracle Moment? There's one. One of many.

"There have been a lot of them," Mara said, sitting in his office, reflecting on a life spent not just in football, but in Giants football, "and hopefully there will be a few more to come."

"WHAT'S A TOUCHDOWN?"

Tim Mara brought something to New York City. He had no idea what it was or what it would become.

The sport of professional football was growing in popularity, and there were certainly plenty of big-time college programs that found their way to America's largest and most vibrant metropolis to bring in massive crowds and help further the reach of the game. Professional football and a fledgling league that called itself the NFL was based mostly in the Midwest with a few franchises dotting smaller towns in New England. But Mara had a vision. He plunked down $500 for the charter that established his team; came up with another $25,000 in operating costs to cover equipment, coach and player salaries, and other overhead; signed one of the world's most famous athletes; and on October 18, 1925, was among more than 25,000 who converged on the Polo Grounds in upper Manhattan on a clear, sunny afternoon to witness the birth of an institution that would become one of the most distinguished, admired, profitable, and successful franchises in all of sports.

The New York Football Giants had arrived.

It was the third game ever for the Giants on that autumn Sunday afternoon. They'd begun their inaugural season with two road games. On October 11, 1925, they lost to the Providence Steam Rollers, 14–0, in Rhode Island, in their first-ever contest, and then on October 17, a day before their home debut, they lost, 5–3, to the Frankford Yellowjackets in Pennsylvania. In an illustration of just how little anyone knew or cared about the game, the teams made the trek from Frankford to New York after their Saturday clash to face each other again the next day.

The crowd was vibrant and thirsty for the kind of excitement that professional football still delivers to this day. And there was early action for them to enjoy. In the first quarter, the Yellowjackets took a 7–0 lead (on their way to a 14–0 victory) when Les Haws scored on a 9-yard run. The place erupted, fans rose to their feet, and Mara knew he was onto something big.

He just didn't quite know what that was, exactly.

As the audience jumped up to usher Haws over the goal line, Tim Mara, it is said, tugged on the elbow of his son Jack to ask a question:

"What's a touchdown?"

Mara didn't understand football, but he understood business. So when he was looking to invest in heavyweight boxer Gene Tunney in 1925 and learned that Dr. Harry A. March had already applied for and received an NFL charter—but could not afford the costs—he jumped at the opportunity. Especially after he learned it would cost only $500.

"Any franchise in New York is worth that amount of money," he said. "An empty store with chairs in it is worth that much."

Just a few years earlier, the New York Yankees had been sold for $460,000, and that was well before they acquired Babe Ruth, played in their cathedral in the Bronx, put on pinstripes, or had even appeared in any World Series. The Yankees were a second-rate team in New York, tenants to the baseball Giants at the Polo Grounds. To be able to buy a pro team for a tiny fraction of what the Yankees were worth must have seemed like a no-brainer to Mara.

But it wasn't Tim Mara's idea to create the New York Football Giants. He just delivered them.

Legend has it that the actual conception of the team occurred when postal worker Bill Findley delivered mail to Dr. March's office in upper Manhattan and the two discovered a mutual interest in football. They'd talk about the big college games that rolled through town, but Findley griped that he could never get tickets to those contests. As for pro football, there was obviously no television on which to watch the games, and he was relegated to trying to keep up by following the snippets that appeared in the city's many newspapers. What he wanted was a chance to see a professional football game in New York, and he told that to March.

The idea was intriguing. March had grown up in Canton, Ohio, and had been involved in professional football there (the city is the home of the Pro Football Hall of Fame and Museum). He was the team physician for the Canton Bulldogs.

At about the same time, the NFL was looking to establish a footprint in New York City. The president of the young league that formed in 1920, Joseph Carr, traveled to the Big Apple shopping the opportunity to apply for and buy a charter. March took him up on the offer in principle.

What he didn't have was the capital to pay for the prized document, so he needed an investor. He first approached boxing promoter Tex Rickard—who would later become owner of the New York Rangers of the NHL—but Rickard's assets were tied up in another project. He was building a new Madison Square Garden on Eighth Avenue between 49th and 50th Streets.

Rickard suggested March and Carr meet with Billy Gibson, who was Tunney's manager, but Gibson declined the offer, as well. He had been an investor in a previous attempt to plant an NFL team in New York when the New York Brickley Giants took the field in 1921. They lasted just two games, the second-shortest lifespan of any NFL franchise ever. (The Tonawanda Lumbermen, based outside Buffalo, played just one game in 1921; they lost to the Rochester Jeffersons, 45–0, in their only NFL appearance.) Having already been burned in an attempt to establish pro football in the City, Gibson was out.

Yet Gibson was in the midst of a deal to sell a piece of Tunney to Mara. That partnership never came together, but when Gibson mentioned the NFL opportunity to Mara, he pulled out of his boxing pursuits and dived into football.

March, the only person Mara knew who had any football acumen, served as the secretary for the Giants from 1925 to 1928 and then as president of the organization from 1928 to 1933.

Mara's initial investment is often cited as $500, but as noted previously, that was just for the charter. The operating costs were another $25,000 or so. Adjusted for inflation, Mara laid out about $363,000 in today's dollars, so it wasn't exactly pocket change. Still, it was a shrewd investment. In 2018, the Giants were valued at $3.3 billion by *Forbes* magazine. The Mara family still owns half of the franchise.

"I don't know that he could have ever comprehended anything like what's happening now, how big the sport has become, how big the league has become," said his grandson, John Mara, now the President and CEO of the Giants. "But I think he'd be pretty pleased."

Timothy James Mara was born on July 28, 1887, in New York City's Lower East Side. His father, John Mara, was a policeman, but the family was poor and always looking for extra income to support the household. When Tim Mara was 13 years old, he dropped out of school and started working several jobs. His first was as an usher in a theater.

Like many young boys his age at the turn of the century, he became a newsboy. He would stand on a corner in Manhattan and hawk newspapers to the folks who walked by. Most of those people were out doing chores or going to and from work. Some of them were on the streets working right alongside Mara. At a time when gambling was legal, bookmakers would be out in public working right alongside those youngsters slinging the day's headlines.

That's where Mara became involved in the profession. He became a runner for the bookies, tracking down customers to either give them their winnings or collect their debts. He earned five percent of what he handled, and often the winners would give him a tip when he showed up with their earnings. By the time he was 18 years old, he had become a bookmaker himself.

"He was a self-made man who was a hustler," John Mara said. "Kind of this larger-than-life figure, a self-made guy who was an entrepreneur. For somebody with an eighth-grade education, he did pretty well for himself."

Tim Mara married Lizette Barclay, and while she was not involved in the day-to-day running of the team, her impact on the organization is still seen to this day. The Maras' younger son, Wellington, enjoyed sitting on the bench during Giants games at the Polo Grounds in that first season, and after one particularly blustery game, he came home with a cold. Lizette Mara knew she could not win the battle to keep Wellington off the Giants' sideline, but she also had to protect her son from future illnesses, so she insisted that Tim Mara move the Giants' bench from the shady side of the Polo Grounds to the sunny side.

To this day at MetLife Stadium, the Giants' bench is on the bright side of the field. Most teams go the other way, hoping to use the shade to their advantage or, more to the point, use the sun to disadvantage their opponents. Sitting in the path of those rays can make it difficult for players to stay cool, and coaches on the sideline must squint against the glare to see the field.

Jim Thorpe was already a football legend when he signed with the 1925 Giants to add starpower to the roster during their inaugural season. He played only three games for the team, making him not just one of the first Giants ever, but one of the first former Giants, as well. (Hulton Archive / Stringer, courtesy of Getty Images)

The Giants, though, are one of the few teams in the NFL who have their home bench in the sunshine for day games. And all because Lizette Mara didn't want her little boy to get the sniffles.

Tim Mara knew that football itself wasn't enough to bring New Yorkers to the Polo Grounds in the chills of late autumn. The fans needed an attraction. A name. Mara gave them one.

For a while, anyway.

One of the first players signed by Mara and Dr. March was Jim Thorpe, who a decade or so earlier had been crowned as the World's Greatest Athlete for his gold medals in the pentathlon and decathlon at the 1912 Olympics. Thorpe had been a presence in just about every sport around since then. He played Major League Baseball from 1913 to 1919; helped the Canton Bulldogs win three championships in pro football in 1916, 1917, and 1919; and served as the first president of the American Professional Football Association from 1920 to 1921. A year later, that organization became the National Football League.

In 1925, he was a 37-year-old shell of the athlete he'd once been, but his name still resonated. That's why he was brought to the Giants. As a football player, he didn't have much to offer.

The Giants released him after three uneventful games, giving the Hall of Famer the distinction of not only being one of the first Giants players, but one of the first former Giants players.

After losing that first game at the Polo Grounds, the Giants won their next seven games in a row. All the games were played at home. The Giants had four consecutive shutouts, avenged their first ever loss to Providence with a 13–12 victory, and walloped Dayton, 23–0. They were a success on the field.

Tim Mara's ledger told another story. By the time December rolled around, Mara was already $40,000 in debt. Something had to be done, and Mara knew he needed a big name to improve attendance at the games. Luckily for the Giants, one of the biggest was available.

Red Grange, the Galloping Ghost, had become one of the most famous athletes in America as a college football player, and he was ready to make the jump to the professional game. Mara headed out to Illinois by train to try to make him a Giant.

A few days after his departure, Mara sent a telegram back to New York with an update:

"Partially successful," the message read. "Returning on train tomorrow. Will explain."

Those back in New York couldn't figure out what it meant to be partially successful. Had he signed Grange or not?

Tim Mara returned home and explained.

"Grange will be playing in the Polo Grounds this year," he said, "only he'll be playing for the Bears."

George Halas, owner and coach of the Bears, had gotten to Grange first and signed him.

So why was the venture "partially successful"? Because the Bears were going to be visiting the Giants on December 6 that season, and Mara knew that New York City would be clamoring to see him in person.

After a week of hype, 70,000 or so fans came to the Polo Grounds to watch the Bears play the Giants. Grange ran for 53 yards, caught one pass for 23 yards, and returned an interception for a touchdown to lead the visiting team to a 19–7 victory. He also cleared a little cash; Grange's contract with the Bears called for him to receive a percentage of the gate.

About $143,000—or most of the money—went to the Giants, though. And while they lost that game, their last at home in their inaugural season, they managed to turn a small profit of $18,000 for the year. It was enough to convince their owner, who didn't even know what a touchdown was a few months earlier, that professional football could survive in the Big Apple.

There were other factors at play in Mara's decision to keep the Giants. For many years, the organization lost money, and everyone knew it. Mara was good friends with Al Smith, the governor of New York who would eventually run for president, and one Sunday the two of them were walking out of mass together.

"Al said to him, 'You should sell it, get rid of it. It's never going to amount to anything,'" John Mara said of the advice given to his grandfather. "His response was: 'I would, but my boys would kill me.' Fortunately, he made the decision to hold onto it."

THE FIRST TITLE

Football is a game of guts and glory. If you want the latter, you need to show the former. That's why plays like the "Philly Special" will go down as one of the top calls in history, a trick play that helped the Eagles beat the Patriots in Super Bowl LII.

Ninety years before it, though, it was the Giants who used some play-calling derring-do from Hinkey Haines, their quick-thinking quarterback, on the way to the 1927 championship. It was, at the time, one of the most intrepid on-field decisions in the history of professional football. And despite being forgotten by many and relegated to the box of sepia-toned daguerreotypes stashed away in the attic of pro football, given the circumstances in the November 27, 1927, game against the Bears at the Polo Grounds that determined who won that year's crown, it might very well remain the pluckiest play in NFL history.

For the Giants, it was their first on-field Miracle Moment.

Consider that the Giants had just held the hard-charging Bears out of the end zone on the opening drive of the game. Chicago fullback Jack White tried to leap over the tangled mass of bodies at the goal line on a fourth-down play from the 1, but defender Al Nesser met him in the air and drove him backward to complete the goal-line stand. The Giants came out in formation to punt on first down, a move that seems ridiculous today but was commonplace from deep in one's own territory during an era when football games were more like World War I trench warfare and determined more by advances in field position than sudden-strike plays.

The Bears, sensing a chance to block the punt by Mule Wilson, crowded the line of scrimmage. It was then that Haines asked the officials to wipe down the muddy ball so that the Giants would have a better chance of executing the short snap and kick. But Haines used that distraction to alter his position as the upback, moving back a few feet into his own end zone without the Bears noticing. When the ball was snapped, it went not to Wilson the punter, but to Haines. With Chicago's burly front line charging, he floated a soft pass over the assault where it was caught by Chuck Corgan, who ran until he was brought down across midfield for a 58-yard gain.

To recap: early in a game that would determine the 1927 NFL Championship, in an era when field position was everything, against a team that had taken the opening kickoff and marched one yard shy of the end zone, Haines called for a fake punt. And he pulled it off!

"Haines called one of the smartest plays I've ever seen to win for us," Steve Owen, then the Giants' left tackle who would go on to become their winningest head coach, said after the game. "He stage-managed it perfectly."

By 1927, Tim Mara had established the Giants as the NFL's main team in New York. Now he wanted a winner.

At the time, that wasn't as clear-cut a distinction as you'd think. The NFL had no postseason or playoff games until 1933, so for the first dozen years of the league's existence, the champion was determined by a convoluted measurement that counted wins and discarded ties (which were much more common than now) and often was not finalized until spring meetings in April of the following year. Add to the chaos a schedule in which not every team played each other, with some teams playing more games than others and some teams folding in midseason due to their financial limitations, and it's no wonder that by the time the 1927 season came around, four of the six NFL championships had been contested to the point that more than one team could rightfully claim the title.

Things became a little more manageable in 1927. That year, the NFL pared itself down from 22 teams to 12. But there was still no clear way of determining a champion in a head-to-head contest. The closest the NFL could come to that was the game between the Bears and Giants in 1927.

By mid-October, the Bears were in first place with a record of 5–0–1. The Giants were 6–1–1, and the Packers were 5–1–1. On November 8, the New York Yankees (the football team that a year earlier the Giants had tried to keep out of the NFL) beat the Bears, 26–6, allowing the Giants to move into first place. On Thanksgiving Day, the Bears lost at Wrigley Field to their crosstown rivals, the Chicago Cardinals.

That set up what became, for all practical purposes, 1927's head-to-head championship game between the Giants (8–1–1) and Bears (7–2–1) at the Polo Grounds. A Bears win would have tied them for first place with two games remaining, while a Giants win made them a virtual lock to win the title.

Mara and team president Dr. Harry March built the 1927 Giants to conform to the prevailing trends of the NFL. They were a nasty, physical, brutal team built on a philosophy of manhandling their opponents. They had two large two-way tackles and future Hall of Famers in Owen and Cal Hubbard. Nesser, who played without a helmet or shoulder pads, was a menace in the middle of the line of scrimmage on both offense and defense, diving low into pileups and pushing the mass of bodies in the direction he wanted it to head.

Just two years after the inaugural season in 1925, the 1927 Giants gave the franchise its first championship. (AP Photo/Pro Football Hall of Fame)

"We were pretty much a smash-and-shove gang," Owen would say. "We were bone crushers, not fancy Dans."

The Giants had a defense that performed to a level never before seen and unlikely ever to be seen again, allowing just three touchdowns all season and winning a record 10 of their games via shutout.

Offensively, running back Jack McBride led the way with six touchdowns (he also kicked two field goals and 15 extra points). It was the dawn of the passing game in the NFL, which would change the sport dramatically in the near future. In 1927, though, the Giants were the best at playing the game under its then-current identity.

"Their line beat the hell out of you and wore you down, and their backs could move the ball," Hall of Famer Red Grange would recall in the 1963 book *The Giants of New York*. "But they would have been passed off the field by the top teams of the '30s."

The fake punt did not lead directly to any points—the game was still scoreless into the third quarter—but it altered the tenor of the tilt and kept the Bears from scoring early points that would most likely have affected the outcome.

Instead, the Giants scored a pair of third-quarter touchdowns on runs by Jack McBride to go ahead, 13–0. The Bears scored in the fourth quarter to close to 13–6 and were marching toward another touchdown in the final minutes of the game when Mule Wilson—the would-be punter on the first-half fake—sealed the win for the Giants with an interception.

There wasn't much of a celebration. The Giants still had two games to win—a home-and-home series against the Yankees—to secure the first-place finish. And a crowd of about 100 people had come out to witness the event. Plus, as the action ended on that day in upper Manhattan, most of the players were just too battered to enjoy the moment.

"It was the toughest, roughest football game I ever played in," Owen would recall to reporters years later after he became head coach.

This was an era when players were on the field for offense and defense. After 60 minutes of battling the Bears' Jim McMillen, who would later become a professional wrestling champion, Owen just sat there with McMillen in the chilly mud, both too exhausted to speak. It took about five full minutes for them to gain the strength to silently shake hands, rise, and head to their locker rooms.

THE SNEAKERS GAME

As the 1934 NFL Championship Game between the Giants and the Bears at the Polo Grounds drew closer, most people thought the biggest problem would be the mud. For days before the game, heavy rains had fallen in New York City. On Saturday, the day before the contest, the teams both practiced on the field, which was more like a lake.

But that night, a nor'easter blew through the region and brought with it plummeting temperatures. By the morning of the game, December 9, 1934, the temperature had fallen to 9 degrees. At 11 o'clock, three hours before kickoff, a crew tried to pull the tarpaulin off the playing surface. It was frozen to the ground.

The players came from the locker rooms and tried to warm up, but they spent more time fiddling with the surface than limbering their muscles. Many stumbled around, slipping on what had become an ice rink. Those who could keep their balance tried kicking and scratching their spikes into the turf in a vain effort to get a grip and try to achieve a foothold.

It was then that Giants end Ray Flaherty remembered the time a few years earlier when he was playing at Gonzaga University in Spokane, Washington, and competed in a game on a frozen field. He told coach Steve Owen that the only thing that helped in those conditions was wearing basketball shoes rather than cleats or spikes. That, he said, had given the players more contact with the ground and prevented them from skating around.

The Giants wound up beating the Bears, 30–13, erasing a 13–3 deficit in one of the greatest comebacks to that point in NFL history.

But that's not why the game is remembered. It came to be known as The

Sneakers Game, and it lives on under that title as a testament to resourcefulness and quick thinking in the face of fast-changing circumstances.

The 1934 Bears were a juggernaut. Having won the previous two NFL titles, they rolled through the regular season with a 13–0 record. Going back to the previous season, they had won 18 in a row. They were a stacked team with talent and diversity, using a playbook that included over 150 plays and confused defenses with wild motions and formations.

Tailback Beattie Feathers set a record with 1,004 rushing yards on 101 carries, with a good deal of those yards coming as he ran behind fullback Bronko Nagurski's punishing blocks. Of course, the Bears would sometimes hand the ball to Nagurski, as well. Steve Owen said Nagurski was "the only man I ever saw who ran his own interference."

The Giants, meanwhile, were far from dominant in 1934. A year after they finished 11–3, their record fell to 8–5. They lost their starting quarterback, Harry Newman, to a back injury in the regular season game against the Bears at Wrigley Field in early November and turned to rookie Ed Danowski out of Fordham as their signal caller. They came limping into the NFL Championship Game after losing the regular-season finale to the woeful Eagles, a game in which their star receiver, Red Badgro, was injured and forced to miss the title tilt.

Still, because the NFL alternated the host of its championship game between the east and west division winners, it was the east's turn to host, and the Bears had to come to New York to play for the very first Ed Thorp Memorial Trophy. This newly minted award would be given to the NFL's champion and was named after the former referee and rules expert who had died the previous year, a predecessor of the Vince Lombardi Trophy that now goes to the Super Bowl champs.

The Giants scored first on a field goal to go up, 3–0, but the Bears were bigger, faster, stronger, and better. Nagurski scored the first touchdown of the game early in the second quarter on a 1-yard run to put them up, 7–3, and then a Bears field goal made it 10–3.

The Bears appeared to score two more touchdowns from Nagurski before halftime. The big brute ran the ball in from the 9 after Ken Strong had fumbled a kickoff, and he also scooped up another fumble while on defense and ran it into the end zone. Both scoring plays, though, were negated by penalties. They also both resulted in missed field goal attempts.

While the scoreboard was somewhat balanced at the intermission, 10–3, the game was far more lopsided. The Bears were in complete control, and Nagurski, Giants Hall of Famer Mel Hein would say, was "three-yarding us to death."

The Giants needed something to turn the momentum. Little did the players know at the time that it was on the way.

Like most legends, the facts regarding the exact happenings behind the scenes on December 9, 1934, vary from telling to telling. What is clear is that someone on the Giants sideline suggested that the best place to find the basketball shoes the team thought would improve their chances of winning would be a basketball locker room. Up in the Bronx, at Manhattan College, the Giants had a connection to the basketball coach, Chick Meehan.

Meehan was a stickler for appearances, and because of that, he had a personal tailor named Abe Cohen, who happened to be friends with Giants head coach Steve Owen and often assisted the Giants on their sideline. Just as the game was kicking off, Cohen was swiftly dispatched to Manhattan College by trainer Gus Mauch (who also worked for Manhattan College) to gather and return with as many sneakers as he could wrangle.

This is where the versions start to differ. Some stories say Cohen took a 30-minute cab ride to the campus, while others say he took the subway. Some narratives have the athletic director of the college waiting to bring Cohen into the basketball locker room. Others say Cohen had a key to the facility and let himself in. Wellington Mara said he sometimes wondered if Cohen had broken into the gymnasium to abscond with the shoes but never wanted to ask for fear of knowing a sinful truth.

However it happened, whoever the accomplice, whatever the mode of transportation, Cohen returned to the Polo Grounds at halftime with 11 pairs of sneakers.

"To the heroes of antiquity, to the Greek who raced across the Marathon plain and to Paul Revere, add now the name of Abe Cohen, the man who rode from the Polo Grounds to Spuyten Duyvil Parkway," wrote the *New York American*.

The next obstacle for the Giants was convincing the players to wear them.

Despite the players slipping and sliding all around the field (Danowski said he was falling before he had a chance to lift his arm to pass), they were hesitant to abandon their traditional cleated shoes.

Running back and kicker Ken Strong was the first to buy into the idea. His first play in them was the second-half kickoff, and it squirted sideways and out of bounds. The Bears laughed. But more and more Giants players started abandoning their cleats for the smoother yet stickier bottoms of the sneakers.

Halas alternated between a strategy of having his players try to stomp on the lightly protected tops of the Giants' feet and trying to convince the officials that the Giants were not following the rules. "This ain't basketball!" he hollered, urging the referee and his crew to force the Giants back into their cleats. But there was no rule about what the players could or could not wear on their feet, so the sneakers were allowed.

The Bears scored the only points of the third quarter on a 23-yard field goal that extended their lead to 13–3. But after that kickoff, the Giants began to find some offensive success. Danowski hit Flaherty on a pair of passes and then lateralled to Strong, who brought the ball to the Bears' 31 as the fourth quarter began. That meant a change in ends of the field to the side that was in shadows. And ice.

The Giants capped that drive early in the fourth quarter when Danowski threw a pass that was intercepted at the goal line by the Bears' Carl Brumbaugh, but just as he was pulling the pick into his body at the goal line, receiver Ike Franklin sped past him, yanked the ball from his hands, and scooted into the end zone to make it 13–10. Still, that was more a fluke play than anything resulting from the sneakers, and the Bears with their dominant defense led by 3 with less than 10 minutes remaining.

It wasn't until the next Giants possession that their advantage showed up. Running behind tackle Bill Morgan in his sneaker-clad feet, Strong took the ball out wide and then cut up the field. The only contact he received was from brushing an official as he scooted through a hole and raced for a 42-yard touchdown that gave the Giants a 17–13 lead.

"Right then, we knew it was over," Strong would say. "We could move and they couldn't."

An 11-yard touchdown run by Strong and a 9-yard touchdown run by Danowski gave the Giants four unanswered touchdowns. The Giants outscored the Bears, 27–0, in the fourth quarter.

The Polo Grounds in upper Manhattan was home to the Giants from 1925 to 1955 and site of some of their earliest miracle moments, including the 1934 and 1938 NFL Championship Games. (Archive Photos / Stringer, courtesy of Getty Images)

"They won it with the sneakers," Bronko Nagurski said. "They could cut back and we couldn't."

The crowd at the Polo Grounds, who had sat through the freezing conditions to see the epic ending, stormed the field and tore down the goal post, breaking it into smaller pieces and hauling them home as souvenirs. Morgan, the tackle in front of the game-changing Strong run, said his toughest assignment of the day was getting through the frenzied crowd after the final whistle and reaching the Giants' locker room.

And the sneakers? They were returned to Manhattan College the next day, battered and torn and unable to be used on the basketball court any longer. They were probably thrown away.

"No one knows what happened to the sneakers," said Amy Surak, archivist at Manhattan College. There is no mention of the sneakers—or lack thereof—in any of the basketball program's records.

The week after the 1934 game, the Bears played an exhibition game in Philadelphia. It was also on a frozen field. Wellington Mara and Steve Owen made the short trip to see the game and gloat a bit. The two men at one point walked into the Bears' locker room.

"The first thing we saw," Mara recalled, "was 22 pairs of basketball shoes and boxes up on top of the lockers."

The two teams continued to play exhibitions after the championship, a common occurrence during that time that helped pad the pockets of the players and the franchises. While the Bears barnstormed on the East Coast, the Giants headed to San Francisco to face some college all-star teams. Eventually they would meet once again, this time in Los Angeles, on January 27, 1935, for an exhibition against each other. It was a rematch of sorts in the California sunshine without the ice or the cleats or the sneakers having any bearing on the outcome. It wound up being the final pro football game ever for Red Grange, who would retire after that contest.

The Bears won, 21–0.

CUFF'S HEROICS

On October 3, 1951, Bobby Thompson drilled a ninth-inning pitch from Ralph Branca over the left field wall at the Polo Grounds to win the National League pennant for the Giants. It was christened then, and forevermore, as "the shot heard 'round the world."

It stands as the most famous hit in the history of the stadium.

The most famous baseball hit, that is.

Because just over a decade earlier, a young defensive back who had stumbled into the sport in college and had yet to gain much attention for his play at the pro level delivered a massive tackle in the 1938 NFL Championship Game that helped the Giants—the football Giants—beat the Packers.

The Giants led most of the game, having blocked two early punts and converted them into nine points to lead, 16–7, at halftime. The Packers scored 10 points in the third quarter and took a 17–16 lead. The Giants regained the edge, 23–17, but the Packers were driving to win the game.

With the ball at their own 35, Packers quarterback Arnie Herber threw a pair of incompletions and then handed off to Ed Jankowski for a short gain. Instead of punting—an exercise that had already resulted in the two blocked kicks—the Packers went for it on fourth-and-9 from their own 36. And for a moment, the gamble paid off.

Herber connected with Wayland Becker for a deep pass that was caught at the Giants' 20-yard line. Becker pulled in the pass, took a stride, and turned upfield to continue his journey to the end zone.

And that's when it happened. Ward Cuff, the second-year defensive back and kicker, walloped him, forcing a fumble with an audible pop that rattled through-out the Polo Grounds and above the din of the 48,120 who attended the game. This was before plastic shoulder pads were introduced, the kind that produce that car-wreck crumpling noise when they meet each other on NFL fields these days. Rather, Cuff's crunch came from one man's flesh and bone and muscle ramming into another's.

Becker fumbled the ball. Kayo Lunday of the Giants recovered it. The Packers never again came close to scoring, and the Giants would score a final touchdown to become the first team to win two NFL Championship Games (their title in 1927 having come via the standings rather than a head-to-head contest).

In a game noted for its violence—the New York Times observed that play was "absolutely ferocious," that "no such blocking and tackling by two football teams ever had been seen at the Polo Grounds," and that "tempers were so frayed and tattered that stray punches were tossed around all afternoon"—the hit by Cuff stood out amongst the mayhem.

"This was the gridiron sport at its primitive best," the *Times* noted.

And yet when Cuff hit Becker, it rattled above all of that.

"The impact," a reporter from UPI wrote, "was heard all over the stadium."

Maybe not 'round the world, but certainly throughout the small continent of pro football.

Cuff grew up in Minnesota and went to Marquette to play ice hockey. When he got there, the team folded. Instead of changing schools, Cuff simply changed sports. He became a boxer. He became a javelin thrower. And he became a football player.

He had a rather nondescript college football career even though Marquette played in the inaugural Cotton Bowl on New Year's Day 1937, losing to TCU, 16–6. Cuff missed an extra point in that game.

After college, he signed to play with the Giants as a running back and kicker, though during his rookie season he hardly did any of either. He carried the ball four times, caught five passes, and did not attempt a field goal in 1937. But he started to emerge as a solid defensive back, and he soon became a key part of a Giants defense that would become the best in the NFL. In 1938, the Giants allowed just 79 points in 11 games and gave up just 10 points over their final five games of the regular season. That included a 36–0 shutout of the Redskins, the team that had beaten them in the final game of the schedule in each of the two previous years, to clinch the NFL's Eastern Division championship and advance to what was then called the "World's Series of Football."

Cuff was described by UPI reports as "a hard-driving back made of concrete and steel" who had been "a virtual unknown at Marquette." Yet after the championship, when it came to recording the heroes of the Giants' victory, it was Cuff who "copped the wreath with a smashing tackle that saved the game late in the fourth quarter." He was unknown no longer.

By the time his career ended with the Giants, he would have his number 14 jersey retired (although it was dusted off for Y.A. Tittle to use a decade later), and in 1976, when the Giants celebrated their 50th anniversary, Wellington Mara would name Cuff to his all-Giants team as one of four defensive backs.

Cuff's defensive hit may have shook the stadium and thwarted what was to be the last big push for points from the Packers, but there were other heroes in the 1938 Championship.

The game-winning touchdown was scored on a 24-yard pass to Hank Soar, who almost single-handedly engineered the drive. First, he returned the kickoff after Green Bay's go-ahead touchdown to the 39. Later in the drive, he lunged for and barely reached a first down on a run that brought the Giants to the Packers' 38. Ed Danowski threw a pass to Soar that took the Giants to the 24. From there, Danowski hit Soar for a leaping 24-yard touchdown pass. The Associated Press wrote that Soar "took the ball off Clark Hinkle's fingertips on the 7 and dragged the Green Bay fullback over the line for a touchdown." Cuff kicked the extra point just a few minutes before his crushing hit.

The Giants' early lead in the game came courtesy of a pair of blocked punts. In the first quarter, Jim Lee Howell, who would go on to become the Giants' head coach from 1954 to 1960, crashed through the Packers' protection, smothered a kick attempt, and recovered the fumble at the Green Bay 7. That resulted in a field goal for the Giants. Howell recovered the second blocked punt, this one deflected by Jim Poole. Per the report from Associated Press, Tuffy Leemans "crashed through left tackle, was hit four times, and finally dove over" the goal line for a 6-yard touchdown and a 9–0 lead (the Giants missed the extra point that was attempted by John Gildea). The Packers hadn't crossed midfield.

They eventually did, and scored to make it 9–7, but Hein flopped on a loose ball to recover a fumble, and Danowski marched the Giants from midfield to the end zone on six passes, the last of them a 21-yard touchdown to Hap Barnard.

Wellington Mara would later call the 1938 team his favorite of all time, mostly because he was 22 years old and a contemporary of the players. He and Danowski, in fact, were buddies at Fordham before they entered an employer-employee relationship with the Giants. Those players in 1938 weren't just Wellington's players, they were his pals, and they would enjoy life in New York City together.

Probably never more than after the 1938 Championship win.

CHAMPIONSHIP FOR A GOLDEN AGE

People like to call the 1950s and early 1960s the "Golden Age" of Giants football. It was a very exciting time for the franchise, to be sure. They were among the first football players introduced to American living rooms via television, they were featured in advertisements and profiles in popular magazines, and yes, they won a lot of games. From 1956 to 1963, they played in the NFL Championship six times in eight years.

But Golden? Hardly. In fact, it would be more accurate to call it the Silver Age of Giants football, since they finished second so often.

Between the 1958 Championship Game against the Colts (a.k.a. "The Greatest Game Ever Played") and the 1963 Championship Game (the team's last postseason appearance for almost two decades), the Giants lost at the precipice of a title three other times.

Those teams were stacked with Hall of Famers on the field and on the sideline, but there was only one moment when they were the best team in football. That happened on December 30, 1956, when the Giants trounced the Bears, 47–7, to win their fourth championship.

It was the franchise's only title in a window of nearly half a century—their first in 18 years—and they would not win another for 30 more years.

That team featured nine men who would one day have their busts enshrined in Canton: Owners Tim Mara and Wellington Mara, assistant coaches Tom Landry and Vince Lombardi, and players Rosie Brown, Frank Gifford, Sam Huff, Andy Robustelli, and Emlen Tunnell. There were another five men associated with the team who would eventually land in the team's Ring of Honor: Owner Jack Mara,

Members of the 1956 NFL Championship team gathered for a reunion in 1996. Pictured here are (l to r) Andy Robustelli, Sam Huff, Wellington Mara, Frank Gifford, Roosevelt Brown, and Tom Landry. (Copyright © New York Football Giants, Inc.)

head coach Jim Lee Howell, players Charlie Conerly and Alex Webster, and trainer John Johnson. Six of them were Pro Bowlers in 1956, and five of them were named first-team All-Pros. Gifford was named MVP of the NFL, Brown was named Lineman of the Year, and Huff was named Rookie of the Year.

In other words, it was one of the greatest assemblages of talent the NFL has ever seen.

So, how did that squad come together?

It began with a million-dollar move.

The Giants had always played at the Polo Grounds, but in 1955, Tim Mara was offered $1 million to move the team from the upper Manhattan stadium they'd occupied since they were born in 1925 across the river to Yankee Stadium.

"If we are worth $1 million in Yankee Stadium and nothing in the Polo Grounds, then we had better look into this," Tim Mara told his boys, Jack and Wellington.

Negotiations quickly began with the Yankees, and the Giants played their first game in The Bronx on October 21, 1956. The deal made financial sense, but it was also a lucky decision for the Giants. By the summer of 1957, the baseball Giants announced they were leaving New York and the decrepit Polo Grounds for California. Had the football Giants stayed put, they would have been left with a vacant, crumbling stadium.

The new address put the team in closer proximity to stardom, too. Most of the players lived at the Grand Concourse Hotel near Yankee Stadium, and they would mingle with their newfound stadium-mates like Mickey Mantle and Whitey Ford, who also lived nearby. It was a movie star life for many of them, several steps up from the dingy Polo Grounds.

The shift in home fields wasn't the only move made by the 1956 Giants. They already had a good nucleus of players, but that offseason, perhaps spurred on by the financial windfall of the Yankee Stadium deal, perhaps trying to keep up with their new home's namesakes, the Maras decided to be aggressive in the offseason. They drafted a 21-year-old guard from West Virginia and issued him number 70; when linebacker Ray Beck was injured in training camp, Sam Huff kept that offensive lineman's number but switched to a position he had hardly played in his life. He wound up as one of the best to ever do it. Then, they traded for Andy Robustelli from the Rams and Dick Modzelweski from the Steelers. Those two would become cornerstones on the defensive and offensive lines, respectively.

Modzelewski arrived in New York with a bold prediction. His brother, Ed, had been traded to the Browns the year before and helped them win the 1955 Championship. When he showed up, he told Howell: "This year it's your turn."

The Giants hadn't finished two games better than .500 in seven of the previous nine seasons, so winning it all wasn't on a lot of minds. But as the team began the schedule with a 6–1 record, the notion began to pick up steam. When the Giants beat the Redskins, 28–14, on December 2, to improve to 7–2–1, offensive coach Vince Lombardi told his players in practice the following week: "I'm beginning to smell something."

It was the faint odor of a championship.

Conerly was flinging the ball, Gifford was putting up great numbers running and catching it (he was the first player in league history to finish in the top five in both categories), and the defense was smashing opponents. In fact, it was the defense that was carrying the team, and the fans of New York appreciated it. Chants would rain down on them from the multiple decks of Yankee Stadium when opponents had the ball: "De-fense! De-fense!" they would shout.

With Landry and Lombardi each running one side of the ball, head coach Howell said his only jobs were to inflate the footballs and make sure everyone made curfew. He likely paid more attention to the footballs.

The Giants finished in first place in the Eastern Conference with an 8–3–1 record, setting up the Championship Game meeting with the Bears. It would be in the same building where less than three months earlier, Don Larsen had pitched a perfect game in the World Series. Perhaps that thought inspired Howell to call the 47–7 thumping of the Bears "the closest thing to a perfect game I have ever seen."

Just like the 1934 Championship Game against the Bears, this one was decided as much by footwear as by football.

It was so cold that the mustard at the concession stands was frozen and the mimeograph machine in the press box seized up. An ice storm had moved through New York the previous night into the early morning of the game. By the time kickoff rolled around, it was a sunny day, but the temperature never got above 26 degrees, and the 30 mile-per-hour winds made it even more frigid.

Before the game, Howell conducted a little experiment. He put defensive back Ed Hughes in cleats and running back Gene Filipski in sneakers and had them run sprints. Just a few strides into his run, Hughes fell on his face. Filipski finished his test upright. Howell gave the order: "Everyone wears sneakers!"

Unlike 1934, the Giants did not have to borrow (or steal) the sneakers from Manhattan College for this one. Robustelli coowned a sporting goods store in Connecticut, and he had the foresight to order 48 pairs of state-of-the-art shoes from Keds a week before the game was played in anticipation of such conditions.

The Bears wore sneakers, too. They had learned from the 1934 game. But theirs were not as good as the Giants' fresh-out-of-the-box models.

Hall of Fame linebacker and tackle George Connor was an assistant coach for the Bears in that game.

"I looked at one of our shoes, and it had No. 3 on it," said Connor after the game. "Honest to gosh, it was Bronko Nagurski's old shoe!"

Nagurski hadn't played in the NFL since 1943.

With Gifford, Webster, Conerly, Huff, and the rest of those iconic Giants able to stay upright on the ice, the Giants rolled to an easy victory. Filipski took the opening kickoff 53 yards, and the Giants scored on the opening possession thanks to Mel Triplett's 17-yard run. They led, 34–7, at halftime on two touchdown runs by Webster, and Conerly poured it on with two touchdown passes in the second half.

"They had good traction, that was a psychological thing," the Bears' Harlon Hill would say. "They were slipping some, too, but we were slipping and sliding around. We saw that, and I think that just knocked us for a psychological loop."

Howell gave Robustelli a game ball. It was in part for his play in the game, but really it was for providing the traction with his sneakers that gave the Giants their big edge in the game. Robustelli wound up giving the ball to his defensive coordinator, Tom Landry.

The following few years would see the Giants gain fame and win plenty of games, but never again would that group of players combine to clinch a championship. The closest they came was in 1958, when they beat the favored Browns in a thrilling Eastern Conference Playoff game, 10–0, then lost to the Colts, 23–17, in the NFL's first overtime game. The Colts tied it at 17 on a field goal with just seven seconds left in regulation, and then Alan Ameche plunged into the end zone in sudden death. Known as "The Greatest Game Ever Played," it is largely credited with spurring the growth of professional football.

The 1959 Championship was a rematch, but not as close. The Colts won that one, 31–16.

In 1961, the Giants lost to Lombardi and the Packers in the Championship, 37–0, at Lambeau Field. Kyle Rote dropped two would-be touchdowns for the Giants in the first half, and Paul Hornung, on leave from his duty with the Army, scored 19 points on touchdowns and kicks.

In 1962, the Giants made a better game of it against the Packers, losing, 16–7, at Yankee Stadium. Their only points in that one came on a blocked punt recovered in the end zone by Jim Collier.

In 1963, Y.A. Tittle tried to win a championship with the Giants but came up short, 14–10, against the Bears at Wrigley Field. Playing with a bad knee, Tittle threw five interceptions.

They may have been the envy of every other team, the faces of football, for nearly a decade. They may have become iconic members of the franchise and the sport, playing in an era when black-and-white images began to arrive in full color, when stagnant pictures in newspapers were replaced by those that moved on television screens, and when being a pro athlete began to shift from a part-time job to something that could bring year-round income through endorsements and other ventures.

They may have even been the wintertime Kings of New York Sports, or at least the closest thing to kings without wearing pinstripes.

But there was only that one year when they wore the crown as the NFL's best.

GIFFORD RETURNS

A 66-year-old man was experiencing some tingling and numbness in his hands in the late 1990s, so he went to a doctor to see what was causing it. The medical team ran a series of tests, and one of them was a neck X-ray. It showed the remnants of a fracture to a neck vertebra from many years earlier that had healed by itself.

The X-ray technician asked the patient a question he would have asked anyone with such scarring: *Have you ever been in an automobile accident?*

The patient, Frank Gifford, said no, he hadn't been.

"I didn't tell him that Bednarik [was] the model of the car, but that's the only thing I could think of," the Hall-of-Famer recalled of the encounter a few years later.

It was on November 20, 1960, that Gifford was on the receiving end of one of the most famous and gruesome tackles in football history, flattened by Eagles linebacker Chuck Bednarik and leaving behind damage that would later be interpreted as a car wreck. Gifford, the Golden Boy of the Giants' halcyon days and the Most Valuable Player on the 1956 championship squad, caught a pass over the middle and started to run with the ball when Bednarik hit him high and flattened him.

"Chuck hit me exactly the way I would have hit him," Gifford said, and he would forever refer to the vicious blow as a clean hit.

At that moment, though, Gifford wasn't saying anything. He was out cold and lay motionless on the bumpy turf at Yankee Stadium. Bednarik waved his arms and shook his fists over the laid-out Gifford, which would become one of the most famous photographs in football history. Bednarik, who himself became a Hall of

Famer, would always insist he was celebrating the fumble that he'd caused, not the damage to Gifford. Gifford backed that up, too.

But the two were simultaneous events, and Gifford was carted off the field with what was called a "deep brain concussion." It ended his season.

"What I had was a spinal concussion," Gifford later learned. "I turned around, caught the pass, and he hit me in the chest. It snapped me back onto the semifrozen field."

At the time, there were X-rays taken of his head, but none of his neck, which is where the real damage was. Had Gifford returned to the field before the vertebra healed, he might have suffered more serious and permanent damage. It wasn't until 1997, thanks to the numbness and the battery of modern-day medical tests, that Gifford learned the true nature of his injury from almost four decades earlier.

"Fortunately, after that injury, I didn't play anymore that season," he said. "It didn't terminate me, but a lot of people thought that was the end."

They had every reason to.

Three months later, in February 1961, Gifford announced his retirement at the age of 30.

Gifford spent the next year dabbling in broadcasting, sowing the seeds for what would eventually become his occupation for much longer than playing football ever was. But he was also surreptitiously practicing with the Giants during the 1961 season. He helped the new head coach, Allie Sherman, by scouting the upcoming opponent each week and then often lined up as that opponent's best receiver in practices.

"There was no contact," he told the *New York Times* in 2010. "I was just running plays as a flanker, what is now a wide receiver. When I ran those plays, I often was beating the starting defensive backs. I started to think that I could do this again. I had been out for a year, but I thought, what a terrible way to have gone out. And I thought if I don't do it now, in 1962, I'll never be able to."

So he did. After waiting more than a year for his concussion to subside, and unwittingly but more importantly for the fractures in his neck to heal, Gifford returned to the Giants in 1962.

Frank Gifford was a star on and off the field. His comeback from a head-and-neck injury forever cemented him in the hearts of Giants fans. (Hulton Archive / Staff, courtesy of Getty Images)

"Look, the one thing that I had loved to do in my life was play football," he said. "I said I can do this, the reporting, television, and radio, for the rest of my life, but I can't play football the rest of my life."

Giants coowner Wellington Mara welcomed Gifford back with enthusiasm, but the medical staff had to allow him back on the field. That took some convincing, but since they'd been watching him practice with the scout team all throughout 1961, they were aware that he wasn't suffering from many physical limitations or lingering effects.

The most important person Gifford had to prove himself to was his quarterback. During his time away, the Giants had changed at that all-important position. Charlie Conerly was out, Y.A. Tittle was in. And Tittle didn't know or trust Gifford.

So the 1962 season began and Gifford was playing, but only barely. He was lining up on the outside as a receiver, which not only made sense in avoiding the punishment of being a running back, but helped the team fill a hole. He replaced the recently retired Kyle Rote (who, like Gifford, had broadcasting aspirations) and worked opposite Del Shofner, altering the way teams defended him.

On September 16, 1962, Gifford's first game back, he caught one pass for 12 yards against the Browns. The following week at Philadelphia—against the Eagles and Bednarik—he caught one pass as well, for 8 yards.

He was on the field, just not making much of an impact.

"Y. A. didn't know me, he wasn't throwing to me much," Gifford said. "But in our third game in Pittsburgh, Y. A. asked if I could beat defensive back Jack Butler on a fly. I dove and caught the pass for a touchdown. From that point on, he trusted me . . . I played three more years and had pretty good years."

Gifford finished the season with 39 receptions for 796 yards and seven touchdowns. The following season, he caught 42 for 657 and seven touchdowns and was named to the Pro Bowl at a third different position. The Giants went a combined 23–5 in those two seasons and played in the NFL Championship both times (they lost to the Packers in 1962, the Bears in 1963, by a combined 13 points). Gifford's production helped them accomplish that success, but so too did his spirit and simply his presence on the field.

"It was huge," John Mara recalled. "My father felt at the time [of the initial injury] that his career might be over, and for him to come back and come back at a high level I think was something that was very satisfying to him at the time. He'd had such a great career, and the fact that he was able to make it back and make it back at such a high level was something that was really very gratifying to all of us."

Gifford retired for good after the 1964 season, when the Giants went 2–10–2 and began slipping into what would become almost two decades of football darkness. During the 12 seasons he was on the field for them, though, Gifford was the brightest star in a Giants galaxy that illuminated the city and most of the country.

John Mara felt that sentiment around Gifford's comeback both as an immediate member of the Giants' family and as a youngster absorbed in Giants football at the time.

"For me, what was I, eight years old?" John Mara said. "He was by far my favorite player. He was my hero. So it was a great thing to see and a really uplifting thing for the franchise."

Gifford died in 2015, leaving a legacy as not only one of the greatest Giants players of all time, but one of the most important figures in the history of the franchise.

His credentials on the field were unmatched. He was named to eight Pro Bowl teams at three different positions, including back-to-back years in 1953 and '54, when he switched from defense to offense. He was an NFL MVP in 1956 and Comeback Player of the Year in 1962. He was a member of the 1956 NFL Championship team and participant in four other championship games.

He totaled 9,862 combined yards during his career, rushing for 3,609 yards. He scored a team record 78 touchdowns and threw another 14 of them, making him a true triple threat. He was inducted into the Pro Football Hall of Fame in 1977, had his number 16 jersey retired by the Giants, and was a member of the team's inaugural Ring of Honor class in 2010.

After his playing days, he became even more well-known as an announcer for "Monday Night Football."

In the half century that saw professional football rise from a sports afterthought to its modern-day heights, Gifford was there ushering it along. He recalled playing "in front of really sparse crowds in the Polo Grounds" when he first arrived in New York and lived to see the two most recent Giants Super Bowl wins broadcast to hundreds of millions around the world.

"It's really phenomenal to watch the growth and be part of the growth," he said. "Having 27 years on 'Monday Night Football' and see the use of television, I have been honored to be part of that."

He may have been Mr. Football to an entire generation of fans, but he probably would have preferred a more specific moniker: Mr. Giant. Asked what he was most proud of in his career, Gifford said it wasn't the records or the comeback or the championship. "I think," he said, "playing for only one team."

When Gifford died, John Mara called him "the ultimate Giant." Coowner Steve Tisch remembered him as "a Giants' Giant."

That was because his role with the organization after his playing days was just as important as anything he did on the field. He served as unofficial ambassador, confidant, and liaison for the franchise and its ownership. It was Gifford who helped broker the hiring of George Young between the warring factions of the Mara family. And it was Gifford who helped facilitate the sale of half of the team to Bob Tisch, whom he knew from the New York philanthropic scene well before introducing him to future partner Wellington Mara.

"Frank was very close with my cousin Tim and even after my father and Tim split apart, Frank would still try to mediate and try to bring them both together," John Mara recalled. "We always had a great deal of respect and affection for him."

Gifford presented Wellington Mara for induction into the Hall of Fame in 1997, some 20 years after Mara had done the same for Gifford. On the latter day in Canton, Ohio, Gifford called Wellington Mara "the father every son would be blessed to have, the brother any man could want, and certainly the best friend anyone could ever have."

That sentiment went both ways.

"I think you can make a case that all-time he may have been [my father's] favorite player," John Mara said of Gifford. "He was a treasured member of our family. My father loved him like a son… For my siblings and me, Frank was like a revered older brother whom we looked up to and admired.

"We loved him."

THE RELUCTANT SEVENTH

Y.A. Tittle wanted to call a running play.

He'd already thrown six touchdown passes against the Redskins, and the Giants, leading, 42–20, were poised to score another one with the ball on the 6-yard line early in the fourth quarter. That's when the 35-year-old quarterback entered the huddle at Yankee Stadium and told his teammates what he was thinking.

They were shocked.

"We were all in the huddle telling the old man, 'You gotta go for it! You gotta throw that seventh touchdown!'" recalled Joe Walton, a Giants tight end who went on to become a head coach for the Jets. "He said, 'Nah, we've got enough points, we'll just run it in.' But we kept insisting: 'You've got to do it! You might never have this chance again!'"

The Giants certainly had plenty of options when it came to catching passes. They had Frank Gifford and Del Shofner and Joe Morrison out of the backfield. All of them were urging Tittle to call a passing play.

"And I'm chiming in with everyone else, saying, 'Come on, YAT, you gotta go for it!'" said Walton, who'd already caught two touchdowns that day. "So finally he said ok. He called a bootleg pass, which fakes a run into the line and the quarterback keeps the ball and comes around the right end and I realized as he said it. I said to myself, 'Oh shit! That's my pass!'

"I didn't want it," Walton said. "We gotta throw it to Gifford or Shofner or somebody. I don't want it!"

He almost didn't get it.

The play was off from the beginning. The linebacker in front of Walton was supposed to go after the run to allow the tight end to sneak out into the flat to catch the pass but instead just stayed put. Tittle executed a fake handoff and started to roll to Walton's side of the field, and Walton wasn't sure what to do: block for the quarterback, who was going to get clobbered by the linebacker, or run his route.

"The only thing I could think of doing was I grabbed his shirt, and I pulled it," Walton said. "He pulled to the right, and I went to the left. I was wide open then, but then I had to catch it. I bobbled it, but I didn't drop it. It was alright then. I felt pretty good about it. But it was a little scary there when all of a sudden you realize, 'Hey, wait a minute, he's going to throw it to me!'"

Tittle never won a championship with the Giants, but he does own the greatest single-game performance any quarterback has ever had in franchise history, and one of the best of all time. On October 28, 1962, he tied the NFL record with seven touchdown passes in that 49–34 win over the Redskins. He threw for 505 yards in the game. The *New York Times* wrote that Tittle "played catch with fleet-footed friends" in the game at Yankee Stadium "as if the league-leading Washington Redskins weren't even there." To put the seven-touchdown outburst in perspective during a time when passing was not a dominant part of the game, Tittle finished the season with 33 touchdown passes . . . which set an NFL record.

Tittle received a standing ovation for the seventh touchdown, and the fans would not stop cheering until Tittle recognized them in some way. Finally, he did. Everyone was thrilled to have witnessed history. Everyone but the Redskins, that is. And probably Tittle himself.

"Well, he was like that," Walton said. "He was very unassuming."

Yelberton Abraham Tittle Jr. played just four years for the Giants. The bulk of his Hall of Fame career was spent in San Francisco with the 49ers. He came to the Giants as an aging but still productive star in 1961. It was during his time with the Giants, though, that he had what became the two iconic moments of his time in the NFL: the seven-touchdown game and the famous photograph of him on his knees in defeat, his helmet removed, a trickle of blood running down from where his hairline would have been.

That picture was taken after a pass was intercepted by the Steelers and returned for a touchdown on September 20, 1964, Tittle's final season. He suffered a cracked sternum and a concussion on the play. He was on the field the next week against the Redskins, tough as he was, but that picture illustrates—and has for more than 50 years—the toll that being a warrior can take on a person. He looks decades older than he actually is in that black-and-white image. He looks feeble and beaten and mud-soaked. He looks broken.

He is less than two years removed from the seven-touchdown game in that photograph. They are such different moments, Tittle's two most recognizable games as a Giant. Yet together they tell a story about how glorious fame can be with 60,000 screaming fans adoring him at Yankee Stadium in one, the precipitous decline that catches up to all of us at some point in the other.

That's not the Y.A. Tittle that Walton remembers, though. Not the one in the famous photograph.

"What most people didn't realize about him was that he was a good athlete," Walton said. "He could run better than most people realized. You look at him with that bald head and you think he's going to fall over any minute. He was in his 30s then, and I remember a lot of times he ran those bootlegs and he'd keep the ball and run for yardage. He was pretty good at that."

And he had a strong arm.

"You'd better be ready when it came your way," Walton said. "He had some zip on it. When you practice with somebody every day, you get used to the way he throws, but you couldn't turn your head or anything or you'd miss the damn thing, it'd zip right by you."

Just like that final touchdown pass on that October day in 1962 almost did before Walton snagged it in the back of the end zone.

Once Walton secured the pass that tied the record for most touchdowns in a game, he had a hard time getting rid of it.

"I tried to give him the ball out on the field and he just kept on running to the bench, so I carried the ball all the way to the bench and sat down beside him and I said: 'Here, take this damn ball, I don't want to touch it anymore!'" Walton said. "I think he was glad he got it once I gave it to him."

Walton caught up with Tittle years later when he was coaching at Robert Morris and Tittle was passing through Pennsylvania. Walton was tickled to know that Tittle kept the ball in a prominent place in his San Francisco home, in his trophy room with a select few other mementos of his playing days.

What made it more significant to Tittle was that it was signed by the entire team. The Tuesday after that game against the Redskins, he left it on a table in the locker room with a pen near it, and all of the players took turns adding their autographs to the record-setter.

"I think that ball was kind of special to him," Walton said. "He was a very unassuming and quiet guy, but he also liked memorabilia and the history of the game, so I'm not surprised he kept it."

A football he never wanted to throw to begin with became one of Tittle's most famous passes. And one of his most prized possessions.

GIANTS STADIUM

It may seem like an exaggeration given the current state of business in the NFL, with billion-dollar television contracts, multimillion-dollar luxury suites, and eight-figure player salaries, but there was a time not very long ago when the Giants were in very real danger of going out of business.

In the early 1970s, they were playing their games at Yankee Stadium, just as they had since 1956, but barely breaking even. Around the NFL, teams were moving into dual-purpose stadiums that were designed to house baseball and football teams concurrently. Yankee Stadium was not. The Giants had to wait until the end of baseball season to schedule their home games, often having to spend the first month of their season on the road. They practiced there, too, which was an inconvenience for the players and coaches. Sure, they were identified with one of the most historic buildings in sports. But they were tenants.

It was time to move out. It was time to move on.

But to where?

New Jersey, where a new sports complex was being built in a swamp called The Meadowlands.

It was politically toxic for the Giants to make the move, not only out of the city, but out of the state. Would they become the New *Jersey* Giants? Would New York turn its back on the team? Ironically, if you consider Times Square to be the heart of New York City, the new building was actually closer than Yankee Stadium was. The perception, though, was that the Maras were moving the team across an ocean rather than a river.

Wellington Mara and the Giants had to take the gamble, though. They could no longer sustain themselves financially as a tenant and with the competitive dis-advantages that came from playing around the Yankees in the Bronx.

On October 10, 1976, the Giants played their first game at a brand-new $78 million stadium that took five years to construct.

"We felt like if we made this move, maybe we can finally start showing a profit," recalled John Mara. "Our season ticket holders initially didn't like the idea. They knew where New Jersey was, but the Meadowlands? The swamp? East Rutherford? Why would you do that? But once they came into the stadium and saw the sightlines and everything, I think they were overwhelmed by it and our season ticket base grew dramatically.

"It ended up being the smartest business decision we ever made."

Maybe it was the red-and-blue seats. Maybe it was the way the wind whipped through the building. Maybe it was the fans who enjoyed an unparalleled intimacy to the field and felt as if they were on top of the action even as they were perched in the upper deck. Whatever the reason, Giants Stadium stood out in a world of sanitized cookie-cutter stadiums.

Because the Giants didn't just play their games there, but they actually prac-ticed there and had their locker room and offices and meeting rooms there, Giants Stadium didn't feel like a building. It felt like a teammate.

"We got a chance to have a really great relationship with the building," line-backer Carl Banks said. "We understood all the little nooks and crannies that gave us an advantage. We knew which way the wind would blow, when it would blow, based on it being a 1-o'clock game or a 4-o'clock game. There was so much we knew about that building."

Some teams call their fanbase the 12th Man. For the Giants, their stadium was that 12th Man. It was a living, breathing part of the squad, no less important or impactful than a quarterback, linebacker, or head coach.

Before each game, the kickers would go out for early warm-ups and get a read on what the wind was doing. That was the first line of information. Then the quarterbacks would head out. When they returned, they would compare notes with the kickers.

"And then," Banks said, "the team comes out and they'd confer with the coaches and we knew exactly what we'd be doing."

Of course, the building would not have been as formidable if it were empty.

"It was a very intimate venue," tight end Mark Bavaro said. "You could converse with the fans. You could jump up onto the wall and go into the stands. They were right there behind the bench, they were right there as you walked off the field. It was really a nice, homey atmosphere."

Even for visiting players.

"I've had many players from the Eagles and Dallas and everything, they said they loved playing in Giants Stadium because they felt like they were walking into an arena like gladiators," quarterback Phil Simms said. "It went straight up, the fans were right on top of you, there were no cheerleaders, there was nothing around. The fans were literally 10 feet from me. It just seemed like when we played there was never an empty seat."

Said Banks: "The charm of it was the fans. When they showed up, it was like 'Oh, we're having a big family gathering.' It was such an incredible fan base in that building, the noise, the intimacy with the crowd. It was great."

The move to New Jersey was not a direct one. In 1973, the Giants announced their plans to move to the Meadowlands for the 1976 season. That same year, 1973, the city of New York announced it was planning a two-year renovation of Yankee Stadium. Mayor John Lindsay, miffed at the Giants' decision to leave the city, denied them the opportunity to play at Shea Stadium or any other city-run venue. The Giants were able to squeeze in two home games at Yankee Stadium early in the 1973 season before it was closed for the construction, but after that they were homeless political orphans.

The organization's first choice for a temporary location was the Yale Bowl. Officials there, however, declined the request. Because of blackout rules at the time, playing in New Haven would have cost the entire state of Connecticut the opportunity to watch Giants games on television (although given the state of the play at that time, it might have been a blessing). The Giants next turned to Princeton, but they were rebuffed there as well for similar reasons.

Things were so tenuous that when the NFL announced its schedule in the spring of 1973, there was no indication of where the Giants' home games would be played. The league had to change its blackout rules just so someone would allow the Giants to play their games. Only then did the Yale Bowl consent to becoming the third home of the Giants.

It was hardly anything to celebrate.

"It was a shithole," Giants quarterback Craig Morton told *Newsday.* "You had to dress in the main gym and bus out to the stadium. The first couple of games there, the fans were kind of docile. By the end of the year, they had baseball bats and were beating on the bus. They wanted to kill us. I love New York fans, and I always loved playing at Yankee Stadium. But Yale Bowl, it was a free-for-all. Everybody got drunk and fought."

John Mara was a student at Boston College at the time, but even having the Giants in nearby New Haven did not help dilute the misery of the two seasons the Giants spent in the Yale Bowl.

"I look at it as just a bleak period in our history," he said. "It was a very tough period to go through. So many defeats. So many embarrassing Sundays. It was just a bleak period, one that I try to block out."

By 1975, New York City had a new mayor, Abe Beame, and he mercifully offered Shea Stadium in Queens to the Giants. They jumped at the opportunity. It wasn't great, but it was light years better than the Yale Bowl. The Giants went 2–5 in their seven games at what, for one year, was the home of four professional teams: the Yankees, Mets, Jets, and Giants.

On December 14, 1975, the Giants played their final home game in New York City. They beat the Saints, 28–14, in front of 40,150 fans in Flushing, Queens.

These days, the Giants play at MetLife Stadium, a facility they built in cooperation with the Jets at the Meadowlands Complex. It opened in 2010 with a price tag of $1.6 billion. The footprint of MetLife Stadium brushes up against the old footprint of Giants Stadium, but just because it fills the same physical space doesn't make it the same.

What the old building lacked in amenities and retail space and suites, in many minds it more than made up for in charm and intimacy and personality. You walk

Giants Stadium was home to the team from 1976 to 2010. (Newsday LLC/Ari Mintz)

into MetLife Stadium, and you could be in any city in America. You walked into Giants Stadium, and there was no doubt where you stood.

"It was a cool old stadium," said Eli Manning, who quarterbacked the Giants in their last game there (a dispiriting 41–9 loss to the Panthers) and their first game at MetLife (a 31–18 win over those same Panthers).

Manning said the thing he misses most about Giants Stadium isn't the building itself, and it certainly isn't the way the wind blew through it. "It was always tough conditions, really windy, especially in that far end zone. It was hard to throw touchdowns down there, fade routes and stuff, so you had to kind of trust your throw. There were certain throws you just couldn't make down there."

No, what he misses most is the name.

"I thought it was always cool to have a stadium named after your team: Giants Stadium," he said. "You always get excited for a new stadium, but you kind of liked it being called Giants Stadium. That was probably the hardest part of it, having to get used to calling it MetLife Stadium. A lot of people still referred to it as Giants Stadium for a while."

Many still do.

Because so much of the team's history had taken place in its walls, on its ramps, in its parking lots, when the wrecking ball finally did arrive, it felt as if the Giants were cutting a beloved player or parting ways with a longtime coach. Or losing a member of the family.

A crane began disassembling the first parts of the stadium on February 4, 2010, after it had served 34 years as home to the Giants as well as the Jets, the Cosmos (and soccer great Pelé), the Red Bulls, and, unofficially, Bruce Springsteen & The E Street Band. Everything from seats to pieces of turf were sold off.

"I had a lot of emotional attachment to the old stadium," Mara said. "We'd had a lot of success there… It was sad. To see the building actually come down, it was very sad. But there are times when you have to make business decisions, and if you let your emotions get in the way, you're always going to be behind. So, we made the decision and it's worked out fine."

That was the lesson of moving to Giants Stadium to begin with, and it wound up being the thinking that eventually condemned it.

Mara's "fine" is a word that sounds drenched with regret. Maybe in this case it is. MetLife Stadium has been a financial success for the Giants . . . and the Jets. But clearly, whatever profits have accrued from the move within New Jersey have come at the cost of the spirit and soul that the move to New Jersey once produced.

Giants Stadium, after all, saved the Giants. That's a debt that can never really be repaid.

A NEW DIRECTION

There was not much Wellington Mara and his nephew, Tim, each controlling 50 percent of the Giants, agreed upon in early 1979. In fact, they were not even on speaking terms. They had separate offices at Giants Stadium, had separate philosophies on how the franchise should be run, and even held separate press conferences declaring opposing directions for the team.

After the housecleaning that followed the 1978 season, a dismal rock-bottom of a year that was punctuated by The Fumble in a game in which the Giants had a chance to win a game but a botched handoff between Joe Pisarcik and Larry Czonka led to a game-winning touchdown by Eagles cornerback Herman Edwards, Wellington told reporters he wanted the priority to be the hiring of a head coach. Tim followed him shortly after by telling the same reporters that the Giants should first hire a director of football operations. That title had most recently been held by Andy Robustelli, but the job had almost always been done by Wellington Mara.

"I'm tired of losing," said Tim Mara, who had inherited his half of the team from his father, Wellington's older brother Jack, upon his death in 1965. "I want to have a winner. Well wants to have a winner his way. Well's way has had us in the cellar for the past 15 years."

The spate of common ground between the relatives and coowners was so small and infinitesimal that when one appeared, it was pounced on. So when Commissioner Pete Rozelle asked each of them to submit potential candidates to become general manager of the Giants and there was one name that appeared on both lists, it was celebrated like an armistice. V.G. Day! Victory for the Giants!

Jan Van Duser would be running the Giants.

The only problem was Van Duser, who worked in the league office, didn't want the job. He had no desire to be saddled with the job of resurrecting a once-proud franchise from the depths to which it had sunk, attempting to do so while answering to two bosses in a dysfunctional front office. Van Duser was out.

It was time for Rozelle to intervene and end the rudderless embarrassment that the Giants had become, not just to themselves but to the league. He suggested—strongly—that the Giants hire George Young as their general manager.

On Valentine's Day, 1979, Young flew from Miami to New York for an interview with the Maras. He arrived that morning with only the suit he was wearing, no toothbrush, no change of clothes, and a ticket back to Florida for 9 o'clock that night.

By that afternoon, he had the job.

It was, John Mara said looking back, the most important hire the Giants ever made.

"No question about it," John Mara said. "George completely changed our football operations, made us a much more professional group. He changed our scouting practices, brought in different personnel. One of the faults we had during that period during the 1970s was that my father was too loyal to too many people. We didn't have enough true professionals in the building, particularly in terms of scouting and personnel. That's something George changed completely."

Introduced at a press conference at Gallagher's Steak House in Manhattan on the day he was hired, Young was not embraced as the savior of the franchise. Rather, most observers were not sure what to make of the frumpy 6-foot-3 Young who had been Don Shula's front office guru and worked with Shula for both the Colts and the Dolphins. He had a marshmallow body topped with a tiny balding head and thick glasses. One reporter said he resembled Khrushchev. Another wrote that he seemed like a tourist who had wandered into the press conference.

If he seemed more like a history or political science teacher than an NFL general manager, well, that might have been because he was such a teacher in Baltimore for 15 years before he entered pro football with the Colts.

But Young was up to the task, even if he may not have looked the part. He went to work overhauling the way the Giants did their football business and began putting in place the pieces that would eventually lead to two Super Bowl championships. He hired Ray Perkins as the head coach (over Dan Reeves, another top candidate, who would eventually be head coach of the Giants). He drafted Phil

Simms with his first pick (over Ottis Anderson, another consideration, who would eventually be a running back for the Giants). Two years later, he picked Lawrence Taylor with the second overall selection. He was in control of the Giants.

He also navigated the treacherous waters in the hallway between the offices of Wellington and Tim Mara like a veteran riverboat captain.

"One of the things George was able to do when he came in was conduct business and do it by virtue of shuttle diplomacy dealing with both, making both of them feel like they were involved," John Mara said. "His communication skills were excellent. He understood what he was walking into. Fortunately, it worked out well."

George Young (left) was brought on as general manager of the Giants in 1979. John Mara called it the most important hire the franchise ever made. (Jerry Pinkus)

Young said he was prepared for the dynamics in the Giants' front office after having worked for temperamental owners such as Joe Robbie, Bob Irsay, and Carroll Rosenbloom.

"Compared to those guys," Young would say, "the Maras were choirboys."

The hiring of Young seemed to signal the stripping of power from Wellington Mara, who had been in charge of the football decisions for decades. And it appeared to be a concession to his nephew, Tim, who wanted a new way of doing things and a fresh outlook to compete in a modern NFL.

But it was actually Wellington who pushed the change forward. It was Wellington who wanted Young, on the advice of former players and confidants Frank Gifford and Tom Scott. But he knew that if he recommended Young for the job, Tim would have balked. There was no way Tim would have approved of any suggestion made by his uncle. The impetus had to appear to come from a neutral party, an outsider. Someone both men trusted and respected.

Someone like the Commissioner of the NFL.

It was after the dueling press conferences that Rozelle called Wellington from Florida, where he had been at a tennis tournament with former Giant Pat Summerall, to tell the Giants coowner that the shenanigans had to stop. Wellington agreed.

He asked Rozelle to recommend Young to the Giants, but to do so as if it were his own idea and not Wellington's. Rozelle went along with the charade. Tim, unaware that Wellington had orchestrated Young's candidacy, was on board with the hire.

It may have been the best misdirection play the Giants ever pulled.

Young's tenure with the Giants was not perfect. After Perkins left for the job in Alabama, he hired Bill Parcells. But he also hired Ray Handley after Parcells left (which he would call "my worst decision"). He put the team in the hands of quarterback Dave Brown. And there were other moves that backfired on him. He never seemed to have a firm grasp on free agency as it became a tool for team building in the 1990s. He made a number of questionable decisions, just as any executive does, and some of them came with wisps of personal vendettas and intangible impressions rather than straight business.

"George was a football purist," Ernie Accorsi, his eventual successor and close friend for more than three decades, said of Young. "Anything that intruded on that incurred his wrath. He was never into the pomp and circumstance."

But what is undisputable is that Young saved the Giants at a time when they were a floundering franchise. In his 19 years as general manager, the Giants made eight playoff appearances, had a record of 155–139–2, and won two Super Bowls. He was named NFL Executive of the Year in 1984, 1986, 1990, 1993, and 1997, his final season with the team.

His thumbprint was on the organization long after he left, too, having not only hired Accorsi, who would succeed him as general manager, but Jerry Reese, who would eventually succeed Accorsi. He drafted Tiki Barber, Amani Toomer, and Michael Strahan, and while he was not around to see them blossom into the stars they became, each of them would eventually retire as the franchise's all-time leader in rushing yards, receiving yards, and sacks, respectively.

"His legacy is obvious," Accorsi said. "It's impossible to pinpoint one thing. He spread his aura all through the organization in every way."

To this day, George Young is quoted or referenced almost daily inside the Giants' training and business facility.

Young retired after the 1997 season due to health issues and took a less stressful job as senior vice president of football operations for the NFL. Three years later, he was dead at the age of 71 after a brief illness.

As much as Young meant to the Giants, they may have meant more to him.

"I've had a wonderful job here," he said. "We've had our ups and downs, but I've never had a bad day."

On December 13, 1997, just a month before he left the organization, the Giants beat the Redskins to clinch the division title. In the locker room, Young embraced first-year coach Jim Fassel, whose hiring less than a year earlier had been met with skepticism.

"He thanked me and he broke down and cried and cried," Fassel said. "He could not talk and walked out. I think that championship validated everything he'd worked on. I'll never forget that moment."

Still emotional and speechless, Young left the locker room and walked out onto the field at Giants Stadium. In the otherwise empty cavern of a building, he eventually made his way over to the Giants' bench, sat there alone, and scanned the vacant seats that just an hour or so earlier had been filled with Giants fans celebrating another division championship he'd brought to them.

He undoubtedly reflected on the journey he had taken with the franchise, from laughingstock to the pinnacle of the sport. Twice. And he almost certainly would have felt he was leaving the organization heading in the right direction.

But on that day, George Young, the man the *New York Times* once said "reveled in his image as a good-natured grouch," the architect of every Giants success in their second half-century, plopped himself on that bench, soaking it all in, and showing once and for all what it had meant to him.

Tears rolled down his face, and his shoulders shook as he sat there and wept.

DRAFTING L.T.

The first things Harry Carson noticed were the rookie's legs. They were skinny and spindly and looked more like they should be holding up a dancer, not a football player. And there were other things that bothered Carson, too. Like the fact that the Giants didn't need him.

"Brad [Van Pelt], Brian [Kelley], and myself, we played well," Carson said. "We had a really good defensive line in front of us. Jack Gregory, John Mendenhall, George [Martin]. We played well together. We didn't need another linebacker, we needed a running back, and George Rodgers was the top running back."

Even John Mara, the son of owner Wellington Mara who was practicing law at the time and not involved in the day-to-day dealings of the organization, recalled hoping for Rodgers to be the Giants' selection.

"We desperately needed a running back, and I had seen him on TV," Mara said of Rodgers. "I had never seen this linebacker from North Carolina everybody was talking about, I had never seen him play."

So, when Rodgers was selected first overall by the Saints and the Giants took Lawrence Taylor, linebacker from North Carolina, the decision was met with a shrug.

"I remember feeling kind of ambivalent about it at the time," Mara said.

Carson was also unimpressed that, when word got out that the defensive players on the roster might be resentful of a rookie coming in and making more money than some of the established veterans—there was even talk of a walkout in protest—Taylor flashed some attitude. Both he and his agent sent telegrams to the Giants the day before the draft telling them not to bother drafting him.

Lawrence Taylor, shown here during his rookie season, made an immediate impact for the Giants when he joined the team as the second overall selection in the 1981 draft.
(Copyright © New York Football Giants, Inc.)

"If he's picked by the Giants, he will not play for the Giants," read the one that landed in George Young's hands.

Young threw the telegram—which would be a priceless artifact of NFL history had it survived—in a garbage can. Head coach Ray Perkins, who'd received a similar message from Taylor himself, discarded his in the same fashion. The next day, April 28, 1981, the Giants made their selection.

Taylor apologized quickly and publicly for the telegrams.

"I don't want to cause any problems with the team," he told reporters after the draft. "I told Coach Perkins that it was a mistake on my part to send the telegram."

But he still had to win over his new teammates on the field. The ones who were sizing him up when he first walked out there, wondering how those lamp-table legs would be able to function in the physically demanding world of the NFL.

"Players, they look at one another like, 'What makes you the second pick in the draft? What makes you so special?'" Carson said.

It didn't take Taylor long to show them and put all of the doubts and concerns and questions to rest.

"He had agility, speed, quickness," Carson said. "When we got into the actual drills, we got to see firsthand why the Giants chose him… He went from like third team to first team before the first practice was over."

And there he stayed for 13 seasons.

Over those next 13 seasons, the Giants would be riding the Lawrence Taylor Rollercoaster. It took them to great heights, including the playoffs in his rookie season for the first time since 1963, and a pair of Super Bowl victories. But it also caused them headaches and embarrassment, as his fast-lane lifestyle often conflicted with the team's goals.

In 1987, he tested positive for cocaine use. The next year, he failed a second drug test and was suspended 30 days. In his 2003 autobiography, *L.T.: Over the Edge*, he wrote that he cheated on NFL drug tests by using urine from other players.

Carl Banks, drafted by the Giants as a first-round linebacker three years after Taylor, says there are three sides to L.T. He divides them up into the on-the-field teammate and player, the off-the-field-teammate, and then the person.

Lawrence Taylor had plenty to celebrate during his tenure with the Giants from 1981 to 1993, but there were dark times, too. (Newsday LLC/Paul J. Bereswill)

"He was an incredible teammate on and off the field," Banks said. And for the most part, the Giants only ever saw those first two sides.

"Lawrence was fun," Banks said. "He was a lot of fun. He was a fun off-the-field teammate. The off-the-field person? We were never invited into that world, so I couldn't give you a lot other than what we read and the test results, obviously."

In those days, the team would bond at weekly dinners at a nearby Beefsteak Charlie's. Taylor, in spite of his fame and the pull of his demons, never missed a meal with his fellow Giants.

"Lawrence participated in all of it, and then when he left, us he did whatever he did," Banks said. "He never invited anyone out into the drug world. But he was fully engaged as a teammate on and off the field. He was a participant in the process of team."

Banks said there were times when Taylor's behavior bled into the team, but those were mostly hijinks and not actual distractions. Like the time he showed up to a team meeting before a game against the Cowboys in handcuffs from a tryst with a woman. No one could find a key to let him loose, so the team had to call the police to unlock the steel bonds.

"As a teammate, the stuff that he used to do that was harmless like breaking curfew or whatever else," Banks said, "he could do it better than everybody else, put it that way. Just like playing football. It wasn't like other people weren't doing it, he was just doing it better."

Taylor played by his own rules. He would come into meetings late and sleep and get yelled at by coaches. He'd wake up, look at two clips of film, draw up what the defensive game plan or pass rush should be, and then go back to sleep. The coach had been there for the last hour trying to draw it up, and he would rub his eyes, say, "Ok, here's what we need to do," and then cut the lights off and go back to sleep.

But there was a dark side. The addictions. The recklessness. The part that went, as the title of his autobiography aptly stated, over the edge. Even after his playing days ended, Taylor continued with a hard-partying lifestyle. He did stints in rehab and was arrested several times on drug charges before getting sober.

Did that taint his legacy with the Giants? Banks paused for a few moments before answering that.

"No," he said. "No."

In fact, Banks suggests that all of the outside troubles actually helped make Taylor the legend he became as L.T.

"I think his legacy, that's built into it," he said. "The comebacks, the suspensions, the adversity, that's all built into the legacy. In the final analysis, he was the guy who willed himself with a separated shoulder to play a game and impact a game. He was the guy who willed himself with bad ankles or whatever it was. Whatever was needed he did it. The flu. Whatever it was, he did what it takes. His will was part of the collective will of the team. He influenced that. His flaws, I think, are built into his legacy."

However ugly Taylor's outside life was, on the field he was beautiful. Graceful. And in a sport where few admit to being impressed, he was awesome.

"In practice, we would sit on our helmets when the drill came up where we had a linebacker having to go against a running back or an offensive lineman or whatever, and it was like watching a show," Carson said. "He would do things on the field that we'd never seen before, and it was all impromptu. He would just think of stuff as he was going through the movements. He was the best that I had ever seen. He was like a freestyle ballerina masquerading as a football player."

"Playing with Lawrence Taylor is the most surreal experience," Banks said. "I've never played with Michael Jordan, Kobe Bryant, Magic Johnson. But I can imagine their teammates would probably feel the same way. With Lawrence, he saw the game totally different than anyone else. He was as brilliant a football player as he was a gifted, physical one."

Mostly, though, it was a joy being on the field with him.

"He made everybody better," Carson said. "And he made it fun."

Taylor retired after the 1993 season with 1,089 career tackles, 132 ½ sacks (plus the 9 ½ he had as a rookie the year before sacks became an official NFL statistic), nine interceptions (with 134 return yards and two touchdowns), 33 forced fumbles, and 11 fumble recoveries. He also left a swath of broken and battered quarterbacks and offensive linemen, and a long stream of outrageous soundbites and ridiculously athletic highlights captured by NFL Films.

Even in retirement, he helped the Giants win one of their biggest games ever. On the Saturday before the 2000 NFC Championship Game against the Vikings, a number of Giants greats attended practice. Carson was there, Phil Simms was there, and plenty of others. Jim Fassel had to choose one of them to address the team.

"I took a big risk, a really big risk," Fassel said, knowing that Taylor could be a loose cannon but also recognizing that even while standing on the sideline watching practice, it was impossible for Taylor to be ignored. "I had to pick somebody, and I asked Lawrence Taylor to address the team. But when he got up to talk, what he said to the team after practice on that Saturday, I couldn't have written the speech better for him myself."

In front of that team, with the members of his teams beside him, Taylor said: "Guys, I'm not here to tell you what we did. I'm here to tell you that we are honoring you guys. It's not about us and what we did, it's about what you guys did and what you are going to do."

"Boy, I'll tell you, that was awesome," Fassel said. "It really set with the team."

The next day, they beat the Vikings, 41–0.

That's the player and the person whom the Giants remember. The one many of them didn't even know they wanted or needed.

John Mara recalled asking George Young about Taylor after the selection was made and his indifference had subsided somewhat.

"He said: 'Just wait and see,'" Mara said.

Young was right.

"I still have never seen anything quite like that," Mara said. "To me, he's the best player in our history."

PROMOTING PARCELLS

The Giants entered 1982 heading in the right direction. They had made the play-offs the year before, marking their first winning season since 1972 and first post-season appearance since 1963. They had a quarterback (two of them actually), they had the reigning Defensive Rookie of the Year, and, most importantly, they had the coach they thought could bring them a championship.

They even gave that coach a three-year extension prior to the 1982 season, setting the course for success.

Ray Perkins was the coach that George Young hired to whip the Giants into shape when he took over in 1979. "He will make it very uncomfortable downstairs for them to lose" is what Young told the Maras of his choice.

He was right.

"When Perkins took over it was sort of a rude awakening for everybody because he was a different kind of coach." Harry Carson said. "He wasn't about smiling and trying to make players happy and all of that stuff. He was a hard-ass coach who really got on your ass."

It wasn't just the players, it was the assistant coaches, as well. He would walk into the meeting rooms where everyone was talking and just stand there until everybody quieted down, commanding attention without ever saying a word.

"He gave this look like: 'I'm the new sheriff in town, don't fuck with me,'" Carson said. "When he took over he brought a different mind-set and a different attitude. He basically reinstilled a sense of discipline into the team. He was hard. He was fair, but he was really hard."

And he was successful.

But two things happened during that 1982 season that no one anticipated. The first was the player's strike, which lasted 57 days and reduced the schedule to nine games. That business had interfered with football was hard for Perkins to reconcile, and he grew frustrated by skewed priorities of the pro game. The second was Bear Bryant's retirement as head coach at the University of Alabama, where Perkins had played under the legendary college coach. So, when Perkins was approached to be named Bryant's successor, he jumped at the opportunity for what he considered his dream job.

Not only did that leave the Giants in a lurch without their head coach heading into the 1983 season, it left them in a strange limbo with a lame-duck head coach for the final three games of the 1982 season. Had they won all three, they would have made the playoffs, but just a few days after Perkins had made his announcement, the Giants lost to the Redskins, 15–14, in Washington.

In the course of one season, they went from championship aspirations to getting dumped by a head coach for a college gig.

"It was a setback," John Mara said.

The Giants felt they needed to name Perkins's replacement quickly. Having Perkins coach out the remainder of the season without the players or fans knowing what their future would hold made for an uncomfortable situation. The problem was, all the good candidates were already working for other teams. If the Giants wanted to maintain some sense of continuity in what they were building—and hire a new head coach before the 1982 season was officially over—they had to pluck someone from Perkins's staff.

As Young went down the list of assistants on the Giants, there were several candidates. Almost none of them had what Young was looking for, though: previous head coaching experience. There was one guy, however, who had been the head coach for one season at the Air Force Academy. Bill Parcells.

"I think he's got a little something to him," Young told the Maras.

So, they decided to offer him the job,

On December 15, 1982, Perkins held a press conference announcing he was taking the Alabama job. Prior to that, he had gathered his coaching staff and told them of his plans.

Parcells, who had run the defense that had led the Giants to their first licks of success, knew that meant one of two things. Either he would be named to replace Perkins, or he would be out of a job.

The day of the Perkins press conference, Young asked Parcells to come to his office for a conversation. Parcells thought he knew what it was about, but Young didn't come right out with it. First, he praised Parcells for the work he had done with the defense. Then he talked about wanting continuity after Perkins. Parcells sat there listening and nodding, but in his mind, he was thinking: "Get on with it!" Was Young buttering him up for bad news?

Finally, Young made the offer.

"Do you want the job?"

Parcells didn't bother to consider the question.

"Yes," he said abruptly. They shook hands.

Perkins finished the 1982 season, in part to give Parcells a fresh start in 1983. Parcells didn't do much to take advantage of it.

One of his first decisions was to bench Phil Simms at quarterback. Simms wound up injured that year, too. Then the other injuries began. Harry Carson was hurt, and the Giants moved Lawrence Taylor to middle linebacker. The Giants lost a 10–6 game to the Cardinals on Monday Night Football, which some people still believe is the worst game ever played on that prime-time vehicle. They finished the season 3–12–1. It felt as if Parcells had set the team back a decade.

Parcells tried to be a head coach the way he was a defensive coordinator, by joking around with and enjoying his players. That worked in a small group of men, and it worked with Perkins above him cracking the whip on all of them. But when he tried the tactic as the head honcho, it blew up on him.

"A lot of players knew him as the defensive coordinator, and that's a whole lot different than how you look upon a head coach," Simms said. "Hey, look, there were a lot of problems in '83, but that was a little bit of it, too. When you become the head coach you're a different person. It's like the difference between how I treat my brother and how I treat my father. I treat my father, of course, a lot different than I treat my brother. I think you need that. There has to be a definite separation between player and coach when you talk about the head coach."

Young started to second-guess his choice and wanted to replace Parcells after just one season. He tried to quietly pursue Howard Schnellenberger, the head coach at the University of Miami, but came back from a conversation with him telling the Maras: "I don't think I can get him this year, but I think I can get him next year. Let's give Parcells another chance."

Looking back, John Mara said, "It would have been unfair to have fired [Parcells] back then because he had almost no chance with all those guys getting hurt in his first year as an NFL head coach."

Fair or not, it was a strong consideration, and had Schnellenberger wanted the Giants' job in 1984, he would have had it.

Meanwhile, word got back to Parcells that Young was looking to replace him. Parcells and Schnellenberger shared an agent, so it was hard for the Giants to keep that information away from him. That created a personal tension between Parcells and his general manager that would linger for the rest of their careers. But it also made Parcells examine his own choices.

"He tried to treat the guys on the team like men, and that turned around and bit him in the ass," Carson said of the 1983 season. "So when we did not perform to his expectations and George Young was on the verge of firing him, basically he said, 'I'm gonna do things my way. If I survive this, I'm gonna do things my way.'"

When he showed up for the start of the 1984 season, Parcells knew it was a make-or-break year. First, he changed the roster. He got rid of Brad Van Pelt and Brian Kelley, drafted Carl Banks, and signed Gary Reasons.

"He revamped the defense," Carson said. "He got younger players who didn't have bad habits off the field."

But he also changed himself.

"He was a different guy in training camp that year in '84," Simms said. "Very assertive. He became the guy we see now. Loud, opinionated, and it was quite a difference, that's for sure."

"Prior to that, he had been a guy who was pretty approachable, pretty friendly, pretty personable," John Mara said. "He changed, and I think he would admit that, because he almost got fired. But we make the playoffs in '84, and the rest, as they say, is history."

The Giants almost fired Bill Parcells after his first season as head coach. He wound up changing his style, winning two Super Bowls, and being enshrined in the Hall of Fame. (Jerry Pinkus)

Parcells coached the Giants to the playoffs in 1984 and 1985, then to their first Super Bowl title in 1986. After a 6–9 record in 1987, the Giants won 10 games but missed out on the postseason in 1988. They went 12–4 in 1989, losing to the Rams in a home playoff game, and in 1990 won their second Super Bowl with Parcells in charge.

Perkins's departure, seen as a black eye at the time, wound up begetting a Hall of Fame coach for the Giants. But did the Giants need to make the move from Perkins to Parcells in order to win? Might they have hoisted the same two Lombardi Trophies—or more? or earlier?—if Perkins had stayed?

"Possibly," Carson said. "We were on the right track. But there were some guys on the team who were sort of on their last legs, and when we went 3–12–1, you could see that there were certain players who didn't necessarily want to do things the way Parcells wanted things done. If Perkins had stayed and been our head coach and Parcells was defensive coordinator, who knows where Bill Belichick would be now? Who knows where Bill Parcells would be now? But Ray Perkins probably would have won a Super Bowl."

And he might have done it without Phil Simms at quarterback. Perkins was an advocate for Scott Brunner, who had brought him to his only playoff game in 1981, and was ready to stick with Brunner at quarterback in 1982 before Simms got hurt and the decision was moot.

That's why Simms says the thing that saved his career was the miserable 3–12–1 record in Parcells's rookie season and the fact that he had been hurt, so the stench of that losing did not stick to him.

"The team was a little bit in disarray, and it helped pave the way to give me another shot to go ahead and play the following year," he said. "After '83, they definitely cleaned it out and changed the team dramatically. Older players were let go, they brought in new people. We changed a lot going into 1984. We had to."

Parcells had to, too.

When he did, he became a legend.

THE PAPER BLIZZARD

The 1986 Giants hadn't won anything yet, but they already knew they weren't getting a parade. New York City Mayor Ed Koch had made that clear, calling the Giants a "foreign team" just a little more than a decade after they had moved to New Jersey and saying if they wanted a ticker-tape celebration for any achievement they might garner, they were welcome to have one . . . in Moonachie, New Jersey.

That would deprive the team of a rite that almost every other sports champion with the words "New York" in their name had been granted, a trip down the Canyon of Heroes on lower Broadway with throngs showering them with confetti and other bits of paper (actual ticker tape, as it were, having been obsolete since the 1960s). More importantly, it would rob the fans of the Giants from participating in the time-honored tradition.

But just like the 1986 Giants on the field, Giants fans found a way.

With 35 mile-per-hour winds howling through Giants Stadium for the NFC Championship Game against the Redskins on January 11, 1987, the second half of a 17–0 shutout victory was played in a paper blizzard as napkins and programs and anything else the fans could tear up into little pieces and set free into the teeth of the gusts whipped around the building to create a snowstorm of celebration.

It was the wind that helped the Giants beat the Redskins, and the wind that allowed the fans to give the team a proper sendoff to their first Super Bowl.

"It was a carnival-like effect," said Mark Bavaro, the tight end for that team. "The fans were going crazy. It was like having a ticker-tape parade for our victory. The ticker-tape parade we never got as a Super Bowl champion, really."

Ferocious winds at Giants Stadium created a snowstorm of paper and debris at the 1986 NFC Championship Game that came to signify the celebration of long-suffering Giants fans sending their team off to their first Super Bowl. (Copyright © New York Football Giants, Inc.)

Harry Carson, who had been there with the Giants through some of their misery, recalled the feeling of release as those scraps swirled.

"For the jubilant fans who supported the team and finally after all those years—especially in the late '70s when people were flying planes overhead and burning tickets and all of that stuff—we were the NFC Champions," he said. "That was big stuff. That was really the thing that made me happy, that we did that at home. It's one thing to go on the road and do it, but we did that at home in front of our fans."

The Giants had no doubt they would win the game. They had already beaten the Redskins twice during the regular season, and while no NFL team had ever before beaten an opponent three times in a single season, the Giants felt confident about their chances. During the week, they asked themselves: *What can they do that we haven't already seen?* They couldn't come up with anything.

Playing the Redskins in the playoffs gave them a familiar foe. They'd already beaten one of those the previous week, trouncing the 49ers, 49–3, and now they had another one.

Any insecurities the Giants might have had going into the game were literally blown away when they arrived at Giants Stadium on the day of the contest. Sure, at first they were nervous. Phil Simms walked onto the field and had to lean forward just to walk into the gusts.

"I'm thinking, 'I finally get to play in an NFC Championship Game, and *these* are the conditions I get?'" he said.

Phil McConkey knew it was going to be a heck of a chore to catch punts in conditions he recalled as "horrendous," with the winds whirlpooling in the bowl of the stadium to send any football in the air darting from one direction to the next.

But when he walked into the locker room four hours before kickoff, he saw Bill Parcells and was greeted with a huge smile.

"Why are you so gleeful?" the stressed-out McConkey asked his head coach.

"Because," Parcells told him, "you're going to catch them all and they're not, because they're going to be afraid of the wind."

He was right.

"[Parcells] calculated that there was over 100 yards of hidden field position in that game because of the punts," McConkey said.

All of the Giants' specialists rose to the occasion that game. Raul Allegre kicked a 47-yard field goal in the first quarter for the opening points in the game, and Sean Landeta, who a year earlier had whiffed on a punt attempt against the Bears at windy Soldier Field as part of the Giants' 21–0 loss, averaged 42.3 yards on his six punts.

Special teams wasn't the only aspect of the game affected by the winds, though. When the Giants won the toss, they did not decide to receive the ball first, and they did not defer to the second half. Parcells knew, from all of the years he had spent at Giants Stadium, what the most important strategy element was going to be.

"We'll take the wind!" Carson, the captain, shouted, pointing to his left, when asked by the officials for his decision after winning the coin toss.

The Giants decided to kick off and defend the east goal. That gave the Redskins the ball to start the game but also had them facing into the gusts.

"Who has the courage to do that in a championship game?" Simms said of Parcells's tactic. "Not many people."

It immediately became clear that it was the right call.

"They didn't know which side of the field the wind was blowing from, which end of the field to pass the ball," linebacker Carl Banks said of the Redskins. "We practiced it. We went out, we knew what end of the field we would be able to take our shots, which side of the field if the wind was blowing across we'd be able to throw out routes. They had no idea. They were just trying to run their game."

Quarterback Jay Shroeder threw 50 passes in that game. Fifty! Many of them were five or more yards off target, altered by the elements. He completed just 20 of those passes. Simms, meanwhile, threw the ball just 14 times and completed seven of his passes. One of them, though, was an 11-yard touchdown to Lionel Manuel. The rest of the Giants' offense went through Joe Morris, the windproof running back who gained 87 yards and a touchdown on 29 carries.

"Parcells had talked to me about the fact that we were going to have to run the ball and run the ball effectively," Morris said. "He said: 'Look, gear it up.'"

The Giants did.

There was no scoring by either team in the second half of the game, but that's when the party started. Giants fans who had lived through the dark ages of the 1960s and 1970s, and had followed the team from the Bronx to Connecticut to New Jersey, were finally rewarded with an NFC Championship.

They would be going to Super Bowl XXI, which was being played 3,000 miles away in Pasadena. This, in some ways, was bigger.

"With the Super Bowl, you know, there were so many Bronco fans there," Carson said. "We saw some Giants fans. But that was the biggest celebration that I was a part of, when we beat the Washington Redskins. We knew we were going to the Super Bowl."

"I think that moment, it was our Super Bowl celebration," Bavaro said. "We thought we were going to win the Super Bowl. But for those fans, I wasn't very

Giants fans used to hold signs expressing their frustration with the players and management. At the NFC Championship Game, they were able to give their team a raucous send-off to the Super Bowl in California. (Copyright © New York Football Giants, Inc.)

aware of it at the time, but I didn't realize how long-suffering they had been before that '86 season. For them, it must have been a great night to just go crazy, especially winning the championship game at home."

This was an era, remember, when there had only been one Super Bowl team from New York… and it was the Jets. The Giants hadn't won a title since 1956, so there was an entire generation of fans who had grown up knowing only misery and pain and embarrassment.

All of that was carried away by the wind on that blustery January day in 1987.

Two weeks later, the Giants did win the Super Bowl. And when they returned, they were presented with an offer for a parade in Manhattan. A credit card company had stepped up and offered to cover the costs to the city for the celebration. The Giants declined. Instead, they held a rally in what they called "the only logical place for a Giants celebration" . . . the parking lots of Giants Stadium.

Besides, they'd already been showered with confetti.

"The Super Bowl is the Super Bowl," McConkey said. "But celebrating in front of those fans who were starved for 30 years in that environment, that was our ticker-tape parade. Ed Koch screwed us on a ticker-tape parade in the Canyon of Heroes, but that celebration was as good as it gets. The torn-up papers blowing, it was insanity. It was so good."

THE LONE CAPTAIN

Heading into Super Bowl XXI, Harry Carson had one fear. And it had nothing to do with the Broncos, the Giants' opponent in that game. In fact, it had very little to do with football. The danger that weighed most heavily on his mind at the Rose Bowl was embarrassing himself by messing up his entrance.

So he kept saying the same thing to himself, over and over.

When your name is called and you run out on the field, don't trip! Pick up your legs when you are running out on the field!

"You ask almost any player, especially players back then, what was your biggest fear right before the game, and they'd say that," Carson insisted. "Because you can't feel the lower part of your body. When my name was being called, I couldn't just trot out, I had to run out and make sure I picked my feet up. The one thing you don't want to do is trip and fall."

He'd never seen anyone faceplant during that moment, but it was still a phobia.

"I can just imagine running out on the field, you can't feel your legs, you stumble or you hit something, and you fall down," he says. "Nobody really thinks about it, but it's one of those things that if you're playing, you have to be concerned about it."

Carson and the rest of his Giants teammates made it out of the tunnel into the California sunshine on January 25, 1987, without incident. The future Hall of Fame linebacker exhaled a sigh of relief. But a few minutes later, that fear of being embarrassed during the pregame ceremonies of a Super Bowl would once again gurgle up from deep inside him. And this time, it wasn't an irrational one. It was actually happening.

The Giants were on their sideline warming up just a few minutes before kick-off when NFL official Burl Toler gave the call: "Captains up!" That was the cue for Carson, Phil Simms, and George Martin to join Toler and walk to midfield for the coin toss. But only Carson was there, and as he looked around, he saw Simms getting his arm loose with some passes and couldn't find Martin.

"So I said to Bill [Parcells], 'I can't go out yet because Phil and George aren't here,'" Carson said. "He said: 'Go.' And I said: 'But Bill, they're not here.' He said: 'Go!'"

Parcells tells you to go, you go.

But Carson still felt it was a screwup. He wasn't flopping coming out during introductions, but surely the entire world watching the broadcast would see him without his teammates and cocaptains and know that he should not have been there alone.

"At that point, I see the Broncos coming toward midfield and I'm walking out toward midfield with Burl Toler and I'm thinking, 'Why am I going out here by myself? Did I do anything wrong?'"

But about halfway on his journey, it dawned on Carson—and the rest of the viewing audience in the stadium and on television—that he was not making a mistake. That Parcells was making a statement.

It was Carson who had been on the team for The Fumble in 1978. Carson who had been through the difficult times. Carson who had been through the changes in the front office and the coaching staff. Carson who had lived through all the hardships that resulted in the Giants reaching this height. And now it was Carson—and Carson alone—who would be standing at midfield.

"I realized that he wanted me to go out by myself," Carson said. "As I'm taking these steps, I'm all excited. I'm thinking about all of the stuff that we went through to get to that point. And then I sort of realized when I looked at the Broncos coming out, they must have had seven or eight guys, I don't remember how many, but for that time, I thought, 'Wow. I'm the only captain going out representing this franchise and representing all Giant fans.' Then it becomes a big deal to me personally because I was that one guy."

The optics of that coin toss remain an indelible part of the Super Bowl XXI experience for many Giants fans. Hardly a week passes without someone coming up to Carson to ask him about that moment. If it looked like something out of a Gary Cooper western, it felt that way, too.

"That is what I thought about, The Gunfight at the O.K. Corral," Carson said. "I'm like that lone guy and you've got Elway and Tom Jackson and all these guys from the Broncos on the other side and I'm the lone gunman for the Giants. Over the years, I've considered it to be a tremendous honor."

It's one that Carson still has difficulty accepting, however.

"Quite frankly, George and Phil should have been going out on the field with me, since they were captains, as well," Carson said. "But that's one of those things that so many Giants fans have burned into their psyche, Harry Carson going out on the field as the lone captain in Super Bowl XXI. I'm pretty sure it was cool with everybody else. Nobody really cared. But it was what Parcells wanted to do."

Why? Everyone thinks they know. But that's something Carson said he never asked his former head coach. They've spoken and shared memories of that game hundreds of times since 1987, but Carson said he has never requested an explanation, never poked Parcells for his motivation in making him go out for the coin toss by himself.

The real reason is far less theatrical and motivational than anyone would think, more a statement about Parcells than Carson.

"I never sent out many multiple captains," Parcells said. Despite having three of them, he would usually have just one or two go out for the coin toss during the regular season.

"I sent out George and Harry several times, but I don't like that six guys out there thing. That's just me. I'm old-fashioned. You're supposed to be a captain. The captain goes. The guy they vote for for captain, that's who should be going. Now they've got special teams captain, this captain, that captain. That's all right. That's fine. I don't have anything against it."

But when he had a chance to decide in the Super Bowl, he wanted just one player out there. Who it was turned out to be of less significance to him than how many there were. Besides, Parcells had already given up on trying to garner any advantage from a heads-or-tails proposition.

"I used to tell officials, 'I've got the worst captain in the league,'" Parcells said. "This is when Harry could hear me. I said he couldn't win a coin toss. He'd lost eight coin tosses in a row. He did. He lost eight in a row. He could not win a coin toss."

Carson did lose that Super Bowl coin toss. Not that it had much effect. The Broncos were the visiting team, and they called tails and won. They received the ball to start the game. Elway ran for 10 yards on the first play. Carson made the tackle.

"It doesn't matter," Carson said of the outcome of the ceremony. "We won the game."

Carson said when he thinks about that moment and that Super Bowl, his mind invariably takes in a wider view.

"I've always talked about that game, not necessarily that game but that season, as probably the best team that I've ever dressed with," he said. "That was really the best team that I played with from the standpoint that nobody really cared about who got credit. It was about us winning and everybody sort of checked their egos at the door. As a result of that unselfishness from all of the players, and also the coaches, we were able to put together a team that was truly a team. Parcells, Belichick, all of the assistant coaches, I think we had 11 at the time, all of the players, the younger guys, the older guys, we were all on the same page."

When it came time for all of that to be represented, there really was just one man for the job.

"NOBODY CAN EVER TELL YOU
THAT YOU COULDN'T DO IT"

Phil McConkey grew up in Buffalo, and when he wasn't playing sports, one of his favorite pastimes was standing in any of the many snowstorms that blanketed his neighborhood, tilting his head back, picking out a single flake as it fluttered and slowly descended toward the ground, and trying to catch it on his tongue.

That was one of the many thoughts that ran through his head early in the fourth quarter of Super Bowl XXI. It was rekindled as a pass from Phil Simms to Mark Bavaro in the end zone clanked off the tight end and fluttered in the air.

"I just remember the ball coming down and it felt to me like one of those tumbling snowflakes when I was a little boy," McConkey said. "The focus that I had at that point was so great and the emotions were so intense that I could almost read the emblem on the ball and see the grains in the leather on the football as it came tumbling down. It was almost ultraslow motion. I can even feel it today all the years later, that sensation of the slowness of it all. It's something that I probably feel and reflect on more than anything else. The slowness of that."

McConkey, who with 65 career receptions for the Giants may be the most beloved catch-for-catch player in franchise history, caught that snowflake ball for a Super Bowl touchdown, one that gave the Giants a 33–10 lead in their 39–20 win over the Broncos on January 25, 1987.

Bavaro said it should have been an easy catch for him to make. "I still to this day don't know how I missed it so badly," he said. "It didn't even hit my hands, it hit my helmet."

Two decades before David Tyree, this was the Giants' miracle helmet catch.

McConkey chuckled at the comparison, one he said he never thought to make.

Phil McConkey came to embody the Giants' blue-collar mentality in 1986, and he made some of his biggest plays in Super Bowl XXI. (George Rose / Stringer, courtesy of Getty Images)

But he does consider that play to be miraculous in one regard: that he was even on the field to make it.

So as Bavaro lifted McConkey into the air to celebrate the touchdown that essentially clinched a championship, McConkey remembers looking around and the flood of thoughts that entered his mind. The snowflakes, of course. His showing up at the Giants' doorstep in 1983 as a 160-pound 27-year-old who hadn't played football in five years while serving in the Navy as a graduate of Annapolis. The first glimpse he had of himself in the bathroom mirror wearing an NFL jersey—number 93, hardly appropriate for a wide receiver—before his first preseason game. The 1984 preseason finale against the Steelers before which Bill Parcells had told him he'd made the team, sending McConkey into a stall in the bathroom to sob with joy.

"That was the culmination of many many years, many many dreams," he said of the Super Bowl touchdown. "And that split second where it happened, even today, I'm 62 years old and however many decades ago that was, it almost seems like a fantasy to me. I sometimes have a difficult time putting it all into reality."

The moment lasted just a few ticks of the clock but felt to McConkey like it went on for hours.

"It's really hard to describe how it can be both," he said. "It's a blur, and yet it's every emotion at that point in your life coming to the surface. It's all of it. It is all of it. It's being grateful to those who helped me get there, it's being thankful to all of my teammates and coaches. It was thank you for letting me be here. You're almost delirious."

For the first time in the Super Bowl era, for the first time since their 1956 title, Giants fans were, too.

McConkey may have been the unlikely hero for the Giants, but there were others who were expected to make significant contributions to the game and also rose up. Some went beyond. One took it to the extreme.

Phil Simms had been peppered by reporters all week in Pasadena. He didn't even mind. After a month of brutal football conditions in Giants Stadium, he was enjoying the Southern California elements. The press conferences were actually rather informal settings anyway. He'd sit down at a table and eat his breakfast while members of the media sat around him and asked their questions.

Friday was the final day of media obligations for the players.

"We're ready to go out to practice, it's no exaggeration the last question anybody will ask me, and Mike Lupica [of the *Daily News*] says, 'Phil, do you realize that no matter how you play, if the Giants lose everybody will blame you?' I remember going, 'Hey, great thought there Mike, really appreciate it.' We were laughing. What a way to end the week. I literally was getting up and he asked me that question."

Simms didn't give much of an answer at the time, but of course he knew it.

"I didn't care," he said. "You know that as a quarterback that if you go to the Super Bowl, if you lose they're going to find a way to dissect some part of the game because they have to pin the blame on somebody and the quarterback was going to be the easiest to dissect. That's just part of how it goes. To lose in the Super Bowl as a quarterback, even to this day, very few guys can overcome losing a Super Bowl as a quarterback and not be in that conversation we're talking about."

There's only one way to avoid it. Simms found that way.

On the biggest stage of his life, the Giants quarterback completed 22 of 25 passes, setting Super Bowl records for completion percentage, consecutive completions (10), and passer rating (150.9). He threw three touchdowns without an interception and racked up 268 passing yards. He even ran the ball three times for 25 yards, including a 22-yard scamper that was the longest run of the game for either team.

It was as close to a perfect game in a championship setting that anyone had come since Don Larsen.

For most of the game, though, Simms was oblivious to it.

"I was warming up for the second half and just happened to look up and they had numbers on the board that said I was 12 of 15 and I went, 'Oh, 12 of 15, okay,'" he said. "I don't know what I thought, so I kept warming up. I didn't realize that I didn't miss a pass in the second half either, until somebody told me when the game was over. As you can imagine, there is a lot that goes on in your head and you're not really thinking, 'Hmm, what are my statistics?'"

Besides the touchdown to McConkey via Bavaro, Simms also hit Bavaro and Zeke Mowatt for touchdown passes. The Giants fell behind the Broncos twice in the game. Each time they regained the lead on a Simms touchdown pass.

"It went well," he said of the game.

The postgame locker room was a carnival. Pete Rozelle, commissioner of the NFL, handed the Lombardi Trophy to Wellington Mara, who then handed it to Bill Parcells. Just moments earlier, Parcells had gathered his team around him and said: "For the rest of your life, men, nobody can ever tell you that you couldn't do it. Because you did it."

The buses back to the team hotel were almost a little lighter than when they arrived. At least two key figures nearly missed their rides.

Bill Belichick, the defensive coordinator, was so overwhelmed by his first Super

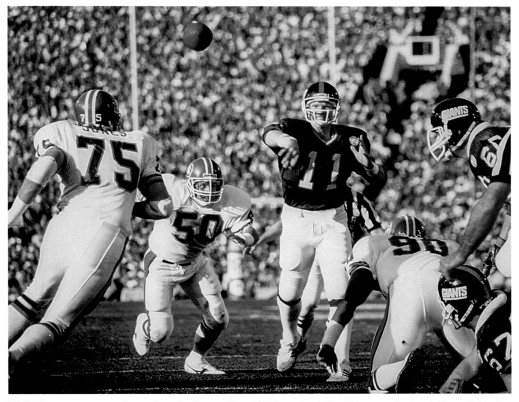

Phil Simms was nearly perfect in Super Bowl XXI against the Broncos but said he wished he would have enjoyed the moment of victory more than he did. (Jerry Pinkus)

Bowl win that he wanted to soak up every last moment of it. He didn't know if he'd ever make it to another one.

So he slipped out of the locker room and went back out onto the field at the Rose Bowl to look again at the scoreboard, the seats, the entire setting. Eventually he tried to make his way back to the team, but security guards did not recognize him and did not let him into the area where the buses were being loaded. It took a few minutes before someone with the Giants vouched for him.

A similar situation happened to Bavaro, who also made a postgame pilgrimage back to the turf.

"It was a beautiful day, probably one of the nicest days I've ever experienced weather-wise, that California air and the hills out there, it was gorgeous," Bavaro said. "But I think I lingered a little too long because I went back into the tunnel to get on the bus and the bus was actually moving to take off. I had to bang on the door to open it to let me in. So I almost got stranded at the Rose Bowl."

While Belichick and Bavaro tried to soak up every detail of the experience, at least one player was at the other end of the sentimentality spectrum. He was also the MVP of the game.

"I wish I could go back in time and feel it again and maybe enjoy it even more," Simms said. "We won. Of course I was happy. But okay, we won the game. I just didn't go, 'My gosh, this is the most unbelievable thing in the world!' I don't know. I just remember that. I wish I would have maybe celebrated more or realized what we did. Only time makes me realize it. But at the moment it was like, 'Ok, we won. That's what we were supposed to do. That's why we practiced hard and everything like that.'"

On a day when he was almost perfect, Simms's one misfire seems to have been not savoring the sensation. Bavaro and Belichick, ironically, would coach and play in other Super Bowls. Simms was on the field in just the one.

He had been maligned for most of his career, booed as a Giants draft pick, and benched by Parcells. Now he was on top, the ruler of the NFL. The magnitude of the accomplishment and the path to it didn't really hit him until after he left the locker room and saw his wife, Diana.

"Her joy was so unbelievable that I remember that like it was yesterday," he said. "Sitting in the stands and watching the games, no matter what, having to listen to people say things about you and 90 percent of it is going to be bad. That's tough on wives and family. For once, there was a good long period of time where she didn't have to hear it. So that was pretty cool. She had the whole offseason and didn't have to worry about it.

"Until the opening game the following year."

FIVE BAHRS AT CANDLESTICK

Matt Bahr stood on the chunky grass at Candlestick Park in San Francisco, looked up trying to gauge the wind, and he couldn't believe his luck. He was about to attempt his sixth and final field goal of the game, a 42-yarder in the final seconds of the NFC Championship on January 20, 1991, to propel the Giants to a win and advance the team to the Super Bowl, when the opposing 49ers did something that he welcomed.

They called a time-out.

"That's about the best thing you can do for a kicker," Bahr said. "Calling a time-out means 'Oh, thank God. Now I have some time.' You can take a deep breath, remember everything you were ever taught, just keep your head down, and follow through."

On this occasion, it meant even more. San Francisco had resodded the middle stripe of the field between the hash marks the week prior to the game, which made the center of the field spongy. Outside the marks was the older chewed-up grass. Kicking off either was doable. Kicking from between them would not have been.

The time-out gave Bahr and his holder, Jeff Hostetler, a chance to make sure they would not be placing the ball in the seam between the turfs and to select just the right patch of field where Bahr's plant foot would land.

As they stood on the field during that time-out sizing up the kick, long snapper Steve DeOssie smiled at his kicker.

"Ha! They think they can ice you!" he said.

To which Bahr replied: "They're not trying to ice me, Steve. They're trying to ice *you*!"

DeOssie's face blanched. Whoever the target of the timeout was, it didn't work. The snap and hold were solid, and Bahr's kick sailed between the uprights as time expired and gave the Giants a thrilling and unexpected 15–13 victory in the NFC Championship Game. The two-time defending champion 49ers were vanquished, and as former Giants kicker Pat Summerall made the call on CBS's television broadcast of the game, he succinctly summed up the transition of power.

"There will be no three-peat," he said.

That was something the Giants had been preaching to themselves leading up to their game against the mighty 49ers. It was a tone that Bill Parcells set in the first team meeting that week when he stood in front of the entire squad—players and coaches—having dragged his suitcase up with him.

"I don't know about you guys," he told them, "but I'm packing for two weeks."

That year, there was no "hype week" between the championships and the Super Bowl, so the teams who won their conference title would be on their way to Tampa for Super Bowl XXV by the next day.

Parcells looked at his suitcase, then he looked back at the team.

"If you're not planning on going from San Francisco to Tampa," he said, "stay your ass at home."

Packing for the long trip and forcing it were two different things. The 49ers were a dynasty, with Joe Montana at the peak of his Hall of Fame career. The Giants? They were a good team, but they had lost starting quarterback Phil Simms to a foot injury the previous month and were relying on a backup in Hostetler to navigate them through the playoffs.

"It was a season for us where we were winning but there were always the 'buts,'" linebacker Carl Banks said of the 1990 campaign. "'Yeah they won, but...' You'd pick up a paper. 'They won, but . . .' Then the next week we weren't supposed to win and it was 'They squeaked by and won a game but . . .' We just found a way to get it done."

They did that day, too.

"Nobody expected it," Banks said of the grueling win over the 49ers. "We shocked the entire football world there."

That they did it without the benefit of a touchdown made it all the more improbable. The 1990 Giants, though, were the epitome of complementary football. The defense helped the offense, the offense helped the defense, and the special teams did what they could to help both of them.

On this particular Sunday, and in this fourth quarter especially, they all fit together like a perfect jigsaw puzzle.

The Giants trailed, 13–9, when Hostetler was hit in the knees by former Giants defensive tackle Jim Burt in the fourth quarter. While the quarterback was able to limp off the field and returned to finish the game, the Giants' defense was furious. And they knew whom they had to go after for retribution.

On the 49ers' next drive, Montana dropped back to pass, and when his targets were covered by Mark Collins and Perry Williams, he rolled to his right to extend the play. Lawrence Taylor cornered Montana, and Leonard Marshall came flying in to deliver the blow that would end Montana's reign.

Montana was already suffering from a lingering back injury, and Marshall's hit broke a finger on his throwing hand and gave him a severe concussion.

"I knew it was the end of an era for them," Marshall said.

Montana fumbled the ball, just as did in the 1988 playoff game against the Giants when he was leveled by Burt. This time, though, the 49ers recovered and promptly punted.

Hostetler was back on the field for the Giants, but the offense couldn't get much traction. They were about to punt after a three-and-out when linebacker Gary Reasons stepped in front of the snap. Fake punt!

"Gary told me in the first quarter, 'Bill, this is wide open, we're going to get this,'" Parcells said.

Reasons would run past Parcells each time he took the field for a punt. Normally, it was a soundless flyby.

"This time, I run by him and his arms are folded, he is looking straight onto the field and he says: 'Use it if it's there,'" Reasons said. "I didn't do anything but run straight out on the field. I am now the quarterback of the football team and take an analysis and look at what has unfolded here for us. Do I call the fake or do I not call the fake? We're really putting the whole fate of the team and season onto my shoulders on this decision."

Reasons realized the 49ers had just 10 men on the field, so he made the audible. Not every Giants player heard it, but enough did to know to block up the middle for the hard-charging linebacker with the ball in his hands.

Reasons rumbled 30 yards—the longest run of the game for the Giants—to bring the ball to the 49ers' 24. That was just about close enough for Bahr to try another field goal, and he made a 38-yarder that cut the deficit to 13–12 with 5:47 remaining.

Even after Bahr's field goal, his fourth in five attempts, the Giants still trailed. And when Steve Young came in at quarterback in relief of a woozy Montana, the Giants still had a serious problem. They did not have the ball. When Roger Craig ran for a key first down with under three minutes remaining, it looked like they might never get it back.

Enter nose tackle Erik Howard, who was expecting an inside run on a handoff to Craig on first down and placed his helmet right on the football. When Howard drilled Craig, the ball squirted into the air and into the waiting arms of Lawrence Taylor.

The Giants were in business at their own 43 with 2:36 remaining but needed yardage to get inside Bahr's range. A 19-yard pass from Hostetler to Mark Bavaro did just that, but there was too much time left for the Giants to kick. They needed to work the clock down. A 2-yard run by Ottis Anderson on third-and-1 with a minute left gave the Giants the chance to bleed the clock all the way down to 4 seconds remaining before they sent Bahr out for the winning kick.

When Bahr made contact with that kick, he immediately thought to himself: *Boy, I hit that good.*

His next thought?

Uh-oh, maybe too good!

"I really fired through it and it was kind of drifting left," Bahr said. "Not outside the post, but it was going that way. As it turned out, that was a good thing."

That's because the 49ers ran an unorthodox attempt to try to block the kick. They had three rushers lined up wide to Bahr's right, where only two blockers were responsible for keeping them at a safe distance. Normally, that wouldn't be too difficult. But instead of the outside player circling around the outside and trying

Matt Bahr watches his fifth field goal of the game sail through the uprights to send the Giants to Super Bowl XXV. (Copyright © New York Football Giants, Inc.)

to dive at the kick, he stunted inside and dived across Bahr's face.

Pushing the ball slightly left—and away from the attempted block—wound up being an inadvertent blessing.

"There is a guy over the block spot, arms extended," Bahr said while looking at photographs of the kick. "I mean, it was just a thing of beauty. I think if I had kicked it down the middle, he probably would have got it. If you look at the picture, he's there. He's right there."

No one on the Giants knew it, though. They were too busy celebrating right after the game, then the next day started preparing for the Bills in Super Bowl XXV. There was no time to go back and break down the film of the NFC Championship.

It wasn't until a few weeks after the game that Bahr and the coaches went back and looked.

"We were like, 'Wow, that was close,'" he said. "'That was on the edge!'"

Those suitcases the Giants had packed for their two-week adventure were loaded onto the team plane along with all of their other equipment. The chartered flight flown by the same pilot who had ushered the team to the Super Bowl in Pasadena four years earlier—superstitious Bill Parcells made sure that Augie Stasio was in command of the DC-10 once again—left California around 7 p.m. West Coast time and landed in Tampa at about 2:30 in the morning in the east.

In between, in the air, the Giants had a huge party. Pepper Johnson was the deejay, playing songs on his portable sound system while the players formed conga lines up and down the aisles.

Even Parcells walked up and down the plane glad-handing and congratulating the players.

"He was like the coolest, most calm guy," center Bart Oates recalled of the normally edgy head coach. "Everyone kept looking at him like, 'Who is this guy?' During the season, he's hard, he's coaching hard, he's working guys… It was like he was one of the fans enjoying it."

Parcells would later refer to that raucous transcontinental trip as one of the highlights of his career with the Giants.

"It was the best plane ride I was ever on, or ever will be on," he said.

When the team arrived in Tampa, they were met by a few hundred Giants fans who had been staking out the team hotel. But the team's equipment staff had to wait to unload and unpack. The 49ers were so sure that they would be playing in the Super Bowl that they sent some of their things to Tampa ahead of the championship game. The 49ers staff had to pack that up and unload it while the Giants' staffers watched and smiled.

"It was, I guess, a mere formality for them," Banks said. "They were headed on the road of a three-peat. All season that's what they talked about. They knew that Tampa would be their final destination as they went along. For us, we were a team that was never really good enough… until we finally proved that we were the real deal."

WIDE RIGHT

The defining football moment of Super Bowl XXV may also be its biggest injustice.

It's hardly spoiling any cliff-hanger to say up front that Scott Norwood missed a 47-yard field goal attempt in the final seconds that would have given the Bills a 22–20 victory. His attempt leaked off to the right, just wide enough to deliver a soul-crushing loss to Buffalo and the Bills, the scars of which still remain in the Western New York city that has yet to raise a Lombardi Trophy.

But to reduce that game to one play, to one paragraph, to the title of one chapter is, admittedly, a disservice to the 59 minutes and 52 seconds of play that preceded it. Or the six months that led up to it, for that matter.

The 1990 Giants were a good team that played great against great opponents, and no day typified that personality better than January 27, 1991, at Tampa Stadium.

Against the backdrop of a country at war—10 days earlier the United States led allied forces in the beginning of Operation Desert Storm against Iraq—and with an emotional and patriotic fuse lit by Whitney Houston's stirring rendition of the national anthem, the Giants took the field against a Bills team that was better in almost every way. And it didn't matter.

The Giants held the ball away from the Bills' potent offense for 40 minutes and 33 seconds, a Super Bowl record for time of possession. Ottis Anderson, the MVP of the game, ran for 102 yards on 21 carries. Jeff Hostetler, the backup quarterback, did not commit a turnover. Nor did anyone else in the game for either side, a first for a Super Bowl. The Giants defense forced the Bills to try to run the ball more than they threw it, tilting the Buffalo game plan in New York's favor.

Yes, it came down to a failed field goal attempt. But the Bills didn't lose the game. The Giants won it. Because they were winners.

They were not the most talented or best team in Giants history. They were something more intangible. Something more blue-collar. They had a never-give-up spirit right down to that final play, they refused to be intimidated by anyone, they relished challenges, and they were as tight a group of players as any who inhabited a Giants locker room.

"The 1990 team," Wellington Mara would say, "got more out of its abilities than any other team I've ever been associated with."

Their Super Bowl win was the quintessential embodiment of that spirit.

And, though they did not recognize it at the time, the end of it, as well.

When Phil Simms broke a bone in his foot in a December 15 game against the Bills, Jeff Hostetler had been with the Giants for almost seven seasons but had started just two games. Now, he was given the reins of a team that started the season with 10 straight wins and championship aspirations but had lost three of its last four.

The season, it seemed, was over.

"Everybody jumped off the bandwagon," Hostetler said.

Inside the locker room, though, there was a different vibe.

"It was a rally-the-troops mentality for our team, but we thought we could get it done," Hostetler said. "Nobody believed in us except for the guys who were inside that room. It was kind of a special time, too. It's one of those when it's us against the world in the underdog role."

Hostetler certainly wasn't about to throw in the towel. He'd waited too long for this opportunity.

"For me, it was a little different because at that time there was no free agency and I had waited six and a half years for a chance to play," he said. "It was one of those things where you'd better be ready because when it does come, if it does come, you have to be ready to perform. I was fortunate enough to be able to do that."

Hostetler started the final two games of the regular season—road wins at Phoenix and at New England—before making his only home start of the run in

When the Giants lost starting quarterback Phil Simms late in the 1990 season, few people held out hope that backup Jeff Hostetler would be able to guide them to the Super Bowl. But he did. (George Rose / Stringer, courtesy of Getty Images)

the divisional round against the Bears. He completed just 10 passes in that game, but two of them were for touchdowns, and he also ran for a score in a 31–3 rout.

In the next two games, Hostetler would account for just one touchdown—a 14-yard pass to Stephen Baker in the Super Bowl—but more important was what he didn't do. He didn't turn the ball over. He didn't make mistakes. He didn't get in the way of the Giants winning the way they were designed to do, relying on their defense and their running game.

There was one group that knew Hostetler was up to the challenge of steering the Giants to a title, and that was the team's defense. They had spent years facing Hostetler in practices as he worked the scout teams against them, and they knew that he could play at a highly efficient level.

"The defense seemed to rally around me," he said. "I felt really confident that they had confidence in me… I felt like those 11 guys had my back and they were going to be there no matter what."

Other than that, Hostetler said the most important thing he did during his stretch as the Giants' starting quarterback was to turn down the volume on the noise surrounding him and the team.

Not all of it was negative. Some even hinged on the possibility of Hostetler and the Giants beating the Bills. But even that hypothetical came with a whiff of controversy. If the Giants had two Super Bowl-winning quarterbacks on their roster, who would they turn to the following year?

It wound up being a critical question in the coming seasons that divided the fan base, the coaching staff, and even the locker room. But at the time, Hostetler refused to contemplate it.

"You just want to make sure you've done everything you can to prepare yourself to be successful and let all the outside stuff, all the distractions, let them go," he said. "There'll be enough of that later on."

In the days before the game, Matt Bahr, whose five field goals in the NFC Championship had brought the Giants to the Super Bowl, was asked several times if he was giving any thought to the possibility of winning this ultimate game by kicking the ball through the uprights. Each time he gave the same answer.

"Hell no!"

He told reporters he would much rather the Giants be up by seven touchdowns in a blowout so he could sit back and enjoy the second half of the game than have it be a close one that would be decided by a kick.

That same question was also being asked of his counterpart with the Bills. And Scott Norwood was giving very different answers.

"All week, Scott was saying he hoped it did come down to a field goal," Bahr said. "I just never really understood that."

Eventually, of course, it did come down to that. Two of them, actually.

With the Bills leading, 19–17, the Giants drove to the Buffalo 3 while chewing 7:32 off the clock, and Bahr kicked a 21-yarder with 7:20 left in the game. That put the Giants ahead, 20–19, but with plenty of time remaining. The two teams wound up punting back and forth before the Bills had the ball to start their final drive at their own 10 with 2:16 remaining.

Jim Kelly drove the Bills into field goal range, their final offensive play being what seemed like a critical 7-yard run by Thurman Thomas that brought the ball to the Giants' 29 with eight seconds left. That was close enough for Norwood to get his wish and attempt a 47-yard game-winner.

The Giants had done just about everything they set out to do in the game. They controlled the clock, they ran the ball effectively, their backup quarterback played mistake-free football, and their defense had held the high-powered Bills to 19 points through 59 minutes and 52 seconds. Yet they were still on the cusp of losing.

"I figured we gave it our best shot, but in the end they were just a scoring machine and they're going to score enough points to win," Mark Bavaro said. "We were never going to be able to score enough to keep them out of the game. So I just figured, 'Ok, this is the way it's going to play out. We gave a valiant effort. They're going to hit this field goal.'"

Bavaro, like many Giants, was praying. But he couldn't bring himself to pray against someone.

"I certainly didn't want him to make it, but I also didn't want him to miss it because I knew what that would mean for him and his career and for the rest of his life," Bavaro said. "That's a big burden to have to carry. I was praying. I wasn't praying for him to miss it, I was praying for us to win. There's a difference. And that's how I got around it."

Bahr, on the Giants sideline, was having similar feelings.

"I was thinking, first, it's a long kick on grass and he hadn't spent a lot of time kicking those, practicing those during his career," Bahr said. "And the other thought was I was hoping for anything else to happen. A fumble, a bad snap, a bad hold, something where he wouldn't have to take the heat. That's exactly what would happen if he missed that kick. I had empathy for him. I wasn't wishing for him to miss, I was wishing for anything else but that."

Scott Norwood's field goal attempt in the final seconds of Super Bowl XXV was wide right, allowing the Giants to hold on to a stunning victory. (Copyright © New York Football Giants, Inc.)

The ball sailed past the upright, about a foot or so outside the scoring zone. Wide right.

The Giants were champions.

The Giants celebrated the win, mostly unaware that they were also celebrating the end.

There were hints. Because of the war, there was no parade planned back in New York or even in New Jersey. There was no White House invitation. Even in the immediate aftermath, there was no real party for the champs.

In fact, their time in the postgame locker room represented their last moments together. There were three separate buses to bring them back to the hotel, where they were greeted not by a lavish party, but by a table with some sandwiches. The Giants may have won a Super Bowl, but the country was still at war, and this wasn't the time to be throwing gala bashes.

"The ballroom we used for the locker room at the hotel, that was kind of our headquarters during the week, and it was a busy place," Bavaro said. "Now it was just a big empty dark ballroom. It was kind of depressing."

There was a little table along one of the long walls, and it was filled with wrapped deli sandwiches. Next to it was a cooler with sodas in it. The players single-filed off the bus, walked into the virtually empty ballroom, grabbed a sandwich and a Coke, and went up to their room. That was how most spent their night as champions.

They didn't even fly back to New Jersey together the next day. Some went home. Others stayed in Florida to vacation with family or went to other locales.

Inside four months, 49-year-old two-time Super Bowl winning head coach Bill Parcells resigned, citing health issues. There had been rumors right after the game that Parcells might leave, but none of the players fretted much about it, because they assumed his top lieutenant, Bill Belichick, would take over.

Belichick, though, wound up taking the Browns job before Parcells announced his departure. The Giants hired Ray Handley to replace Parcells.

"That was officially the end," Carl Banks said. "It just didn't feel the same anymore. The decisions that were made in the coaching area just, they just didn't sync up with the type of players we were. Some of it was change for the sake of change. Some of it was ego because you had new coaches who wanted to prove that they were better than Bill Belichick or Bill Parcells. It just didn't work."

It wasn't just the coaches. Players who had been part of the identity of the championship teams also left.

One of them was Bavaro, who required knee surgery and knew he would never again be playing for the Giants.

"The Giants and the doctors were telling me my career was over, and I had no reason to doubt them," he said. "I figured my career was over after that Super

Lawrence Taylor and Carl Banks carry Bill Parcells off the field following Super Bowl XXV, a game that also marked the end of an era for the franchise. (Copyright © New York Football Giants, Inc.)

Bowl, and I do remember thinking, 'What a great way for it to end.' I mean, how many guys get to end their career with the last game they ever play in a Super Bowl and you win it? I was very happy and grateful, but sad at the same time. It was a bittersweet moment for me."

That Bavaro was able to continue playing in the NFL—with the Browns in 1992 and then two years with the Eagles—made it more bitter than sweet.

"Looking back, we were dominant," Bavaro said. "We beat the shit out of people, we dominated games, we held the ball and ran the ball down people's throats. Our defense was a little older, but we had Hall of Fame players and some of the greatest defensive players ever. To go from that to almost total disarray the next year, it was sad to watch. Thankfully I didn't have to watch it up close."

The Giants went 8–8 in 1991, 6–10 in 1992, Handley's only two seasons as head coach.

Bavaro did get to see a glimpse of the rubble. The Browns and Giants practiced together in training camp in 1992, the summer Bavaro returned to football following his knee surgery.

"I saw a lot of the changes firsthand," he said. "I saw the attitude change, the discipline change. A lot of new faces. It was like 'The Twilight Zone' for me. I recognized a lot of things, but it was not what I remembered. 'What's happened to this place?' It was sad. It was sad."

He added that it made him glad to have been dumped by the Giants and finish his career elsewhere.

"If you're going to go through mediocrity, do it somewhere that is unfamiliar so it doesn't really mean that much to you," he said.

Super Bowl XXV is often remembered as one of the most dramatic endings in football history. For many Giants, it has nothing to do with Scott Norwood.

"After that game when Lawrence [Taylor] and I gave Parcells a ride on our shoulders, I kind of knew that was it for him," Banks said. "I kind of knew that was it for him. What I didn't know was that would be it for the type of football that we wanted to play."

ENTER TISCH

Bob Tisch had known Art Modell for many years. Their businesses and philanthropic ventures had helped forge a friendship. Modell was the owner of the Cleveland Browns (this was before pulling up stakes and moving the franchise to Baltimore to become the Ravens) but did a lot of business in New York City. He was even a Giants season ticket holder, often taking associates to those games. Tisch was the owner of the Loews hotel and theater chain and served as the postmaster general. He and his wife, Joan, were very involved in a number of causes in the New York area. And yes, he too was a Giants season ticket holder.

The two men had many conversations over the years about a variety of topics, but one subject that often came up was football.

They'd talk about the NFL, about the Giants—the team that both men grew up rooting for—and about the sport in general. They'd discuss the history of the game and its future. They'd talk as fans.

Then, one day, Modell called Tisch with a question.

"Would you like to buy a football team?"

Tisch's first response was to ask if Modell was selling the Browns.

"No," Modell said. "But let's have lunch."

It was at that meeting that Modell set forth the framework for what would eventually—and relatively quickly—become Tisch's 50 percent ownership stake in the New York Giants.

There were essentially two conditions that were set forth at that meal. The first was a nonnegotiable price for the half of the franchise that was being sold by Tim Mara, around $75 million. Tisch didn't blink. The second was that there would have to be a successful agreement with Wellington Mara, who was maintaining his 50 percent share of the organization, regarding the roles each would play in terms of running the team. With a 50–50 split, there'd have to be rules about things like who had the power to hire and fire coaches, who would vote at league meetings, and other such matters.

"As I remember, my father's response was: I have no concerns that I will quickly be able to work out the management and coownership agreement with him," said his son, Steve Tisch, now the chairman and executive vice-president—coowner, for short—of the Giants.

Those negotiations did move swiftly.

John Mara, Wellington's son and now president and CEO of the Giants, played a very large role in the agreement between the two men thanks to his knowledge of the football business as well as his schooling as an attorney.

On the day before the Giants played the Bills in Super Bowl XXV, John Mara went to Bob Tisch's hotel suite in Tampa. He had come to town as a fan for the big game. He left as something much more than that.

"We ironed out the last couple of details and shook hands, and that was pretty much it," Mara said. "It was always a very friendly negotiation. Not all of them are, but this one was."

The agreement was in place. Pending approval from the league that spring, Bob Tisch owned half of the team that was playing in and would win the Super Bowl in the next 24 hours.

Not a bad way to start out in the business.

Tisch purchased half of the franchise from Tim Mara, the grandson of the team's founder. He had inherited his share from his father, Jack, who was the brother of Wellington Mara. Jack passed away in 1965.

Wellington and Tim had a dysfunctional relationship as coowners of the Giants.

"The public feud that my father and cousin had was a particularly painful period," John Mara said. "It was tabloid back pages—and sometimes front pages— for quite a long period of time. They were holding dueling press conferences. It was an ugly, ugly scene."

Tim Mara considered selling his half of the team at several points, including in 1984 and 1986. "I just felt like at this point in my life the time was right," Tim Mara said at the time of the sale.

As for Tisch, he certainly had the financial wherewithal to purchase an entire team had such an opportunity come about. And there were a few times before the Giants deal came together that he did put out feelers—or receive them—regarding a team that was on the market.

"My father, as he became more successful, really had a dream that he someday could possibly own a professional sports team in a city that he loved," Steve Tisch said. "When he received the phone call about the Giants, for my father, it was truly a dream come true... I believe that for my father, 50 percent of the New York Giants was much more important to him than 100 percent of any of the other NFL teams. He was Mr. New York. When the opportunity to buy 50 percent of the New York Giants was offered, there was no way he was going to say, 'Let me think about it,' or 'I'd rather own 100 percent of another NFL team.' For him it was an answered prayer. He was very, very excited."

Preston Robert Tisch, whom everyone called Bob, bought half of the Giants in 1991. His family still controls 50 percent of the franchise. (Jerry Pinkus)

The Giants became—and remain—the only professional sports team with a true 50–50 split in ownership. That has led to some interesting situations over the years.

For instance, one of the first things Tisch noticed in going over the team's books was the expense of providing lunch for all of the organization's employees.

"That goes back to my grandfather's day when there were eight employees in Manhattan," John Mara said. "I remember him looking at some of our expense reports and he asked about it and I told him about it and he looked at me with horror. He said, 'Nobody does that! Why do you do that?'"

Mara explained not only the convention, but the practicality of it. With the offices in the Meadowlands, there were not a lot of nearby options for picking up a quick midday bite. Mara told Tisch it was a practice he and his family would like to continue.

"He went along with it," Mara said. "He saw that there were certain traditions that we had, and he didn't want to interfere with those. That's something I'll always appreciate about him."

There were other areas where Tisch's business acumen was heeded.

"He knew what he didn't know, so he didn't come in and start giving advice about who to play or things like that," Mara said. "But he was very opinionated about some of our business practices, and he helped us a great deal. I like to say he professionalized us in terms of some of our business practices back then, made us more of a properly run business. We've always been kind of a mom-and-pop operation, and to a certain extent we still are, but there were practices he helped us implement, financial practices, that have served us very well."

Preston Robert Tisch, whom everyone called Bob, was born to Sadye and Al Tisch in Bensonhurst, Brooklyn, on April 29, 1926. He went to the University of Michigan—where he met his wife, Joan—and in 1946 with his brother Laurence opened a hotel. That partnership eventually grew into ownership of Loews Inc. in 1959 and the creating of Loews Theaters and Loews Hotels in 1970.

His position with the company took him around the world, but he always remained a New Yorker at heart. And a Giants fan. He and his family spent time living in Miami and Atlantic City before returning to Manhattan in 1959. One of their first purchases upon rerooting in the Big Apple was season tickets for the Giants at Yankee Stadium.

Bob Tisch ran his businesses with an employee-first attitude. At one point, he personally hired all of the bellhops in his hotels, seeing them as his best salesmen because they were in immediate contact with the customers. He never took himself or his success so seriously that he made himself inaccessible. It was often said that Bob Tisch was as comfortable talking to the guest in the penthouse at the Regency as he was with the housekeepers, the bellmen, and the doormen.

And when it came to the Giants, that was accurate, as well.

When Tisch died, a memorial service was held at Avery Fisher Hall. Bob's son Jonathan, now the treasurer for the Giants, asked running back Tiki Barber to say a few words at the event.

Barber was nervous, not by the size of the audience, but by the stature of it.

"It was New York politicians, media executives, billionaires, really a who's who," Barber said. "And I'm speaking. I didn't write anything. I remember having a conversation with Jon asking him, 'What do I say?' He said: 'Just tell us how you feel about Bob.' So I didn't write anything, I just went up there and started talking."

The ceremony was solemn. There were very few reactions to what people were saying as they shared profound and deeply meaningful stories about their relationships with Bob Tisch. Barber took the stage in that somber setting and began talking about all the things he knew about Tisch, his role as postmaster, his various businesses. Basically the Wikipedia version of the man's life.

"And then I said: 'But to me, Bob's greatest accomplishment was that he made a young black guy from rural Virginia feel like he was Jewish in New York City,'" Barber said. "And everybody started cracking up. But that's how I felt about him."

That's the way Bob Tisch wanted everyone to feel about him.

They say when you marry a person, you don't only marry them, but you marry their whole family. The same is true of buying or selling half an NFL team. While Wellington Mara and Bob Tisch knew each other casually and had many mutual friends including Art Modell, Paul Tagliabue, and even Frank Gifford, their sons were complete strangers.

In 2005, they became partners.

Wellington Mara died on October 25 of that year. John Mara took over control of the Mara half of the organization, which was no surprise. As Wellington's oldest son and a longtime officer in the organization, he had been groomed for the position over the course of his lifetime. But when Bob Tisch died on November 15, it was unclear who would take over for him in the Giants' hierarchy. At least not publicly.

Steve Tisch was a successful movie producer in Los Angeles and seemed the least likely of Tisch's three children to be in line for the job. But in early August of 2004, when Bob Tisch was diagnosed with brain cancer, Steve Tisch moved from California back to New York to be with him.

"I remember walking into his room at NYU Hospital probably 36 hours after his diagnosis because I wanted to be with my father, with my family, with my siblings," Steve Tisch said. "And I made a promise to my father and my mother, to my siblings, to my kids who were a lot younger then, and to myself, that I was going to be with my father and with my family in New York."

Bob Tisch lived another 16 months and remained heavily involved in the business of the Giants. He wanted to be at his office and part of meetings with the Maras, the front office, the coaches. And he asked his son Steve to join him.

"In many ways, I felt like I was a teenager going to work with his dad, but that's exactly what it was like," Steve Tisch said.

The two spent time together in the office at Giants Stadium, Steve watching how his father navigated his role and absorbing lessons on a daily basis. It was a crash course on NFL ownership. And at one point during that 16-month period, the question all of it had been leading toward was asked.

"When I am no longer able to represent my ownership and our family's ownership of the New York Giants," Bob Tisch said to Steve, "will you do that for me and for your family?"

"I mean, it was a very emotional request, a very heartwarming and heartbreaking request," Steve Tisch recalled of the moment. "And of course I said I would be honored to. And I did."

When Bob Tisch died, John Mara and Steve Tisch, two very different personalities brought up in very different ways and in very different family-run businesses, were thrust into a partnership.

"The foundation of my relationship with John is totally built on trust," Steve Tisch said. "John is the president of the New York Giants, John clearly has the Giants and the NFL in his DNA, and I've learned quite a bit observing John, being John's partner."

And what does Tisch bring?

"I think my experience of 45-plus years spent in the entertainment business, John appreciates and realizes that that brings a lot to an NFL team in modern times," he said. "There is very little difference between the seats in a movie theater and the seats in a football stadium. The product is either on the screen or on the field, and whether it's the players who play for the New York Giants or the movie an audience is watching, if it works and engages the fans, you're going to have success."

The Giants have. John Mara and Steve Tisch have won two Super Bowls together, two more than their fathers did during their 14-year partnership.

"Whenever you enter into a relationship like this, it's always a bit of a gamble," John Mara said. "You never know for sure. Fortunately, it's worked out. It's exceeded my expectations."

Other than the 1990 Giants team that won Super Bowl XXV, which came just a day after the two families had a handshake agreement on their partnership, Wellington Mara and Bob Tisch did officially coown one team that made it to the Super Bowl. The 2000 Giants played in the big game… and faced a Ravens team that was owned by their old friend Art Modell.

"This [Super Bowl] is great for everybody," Bob Tisch said during that week before the game in Tampa, the same city where he had initially finalized the deal a decade earlier. "It's great for the Modell family, the Mara family, and the Tisch family."

Tisch said when he bought his share of the Giants he told Wellington Mara that he wanted "10 years of pleasure" from the experience. Wellington Mara's response to him was that it would take 30 years to get 10 years of pleasure.

"I'm kidding him now that we did it in nine years after I came to the team," Tisch joked at that Super Bowl.

He never got to raise a Lombardi Trophy himself. He's the only owner or coowner of the Giants who has never (officially) won a championship.

But he may have extruded more pleasure from his role—certainly more than 10 years' worth—than anyone who has ever held that position with the franchise.

THE GUARANTEE

Jim Fassel's midweek news conferences were typically snoozy affairs. The soft-spoken head coach would summarize the injuries, talk a bit about the upcoming opponent, maybe share some details from the game plan… but not enough of them to make any headlines. So when Fassel, head coach of a Giants team that had started the season 7–2 but had lost the last two games to fall to 7–4, strode into the media room in the basement of Giants Stadium and stepped behind a lectern with a microphone poking out from its top on November 22, 2000, few people expected anything significant to emerge.

Certainly not the Giants' management, which was already considering how much longer Fassel would be on the job for them, not to mention how they would be spending the Thanksgiving holiday the following day.

Yet a few minutes after completing his media obligation, a brash, wide-eyed, pumped-up Fassel walked up to the suite of offices on the second floor of the stadium, barged into the room where team President John Mara and General Manager Ernie Accorsi were sitting, and told them:

"Well, I did it."

The two men who made the most important decisions in the organization looked at each other with the same question: *Did what?* They hadn't been paying attention to the press conference. They had no idea what he was talking about.

"I guaranteed we're going to the playoffs," Fassel said.

And with that, he left the office and began his quest to make good on his promise.

It wasn't a spur-of-the-moment, blurt-it-out, oh-crap-I-said-it-now-I-have-to-deliver guarantee that Fassel made. In fact, the idea popped into his head the night before he made the public declaration.

"We had lost to Detroit (31–21 on November 19) and there was going to be a lot of stuff going on about the Giants not getting it done, and I wanted to take care of it," Fassel said. "I remember I was in my office late and I said, 'I gotta figure out a way to get this turned around.' I called [Giants director of communications] Pat Hanlon, it was probably 10 or 11 o'clock, and I told him that I'm going to guarantee that we're going to the playoffs."

"You're putting your job on the line," Hanlon told him.

"Pat," Fassel replied, "my job is always on the line."

After that, it was just a matter of telling the rest of the world.

The first group he told was his coaching staff. He called a meeting of them at around 11 p.m. that night, pulling them away from their typical Tuesday responsibilities of game-planning the upcoming opponent. He told them that the following day he would publicly guarantee a playoff berth.

"And there was no sound," Fassel said.

Next to know were the players.

He told them about his guarantee on Wednesday morning, and to add juice to his statement, he also told them that he had cut the special teams MVP from a season earlier, Bashir Levingston. Levingston had fumbled a kickoff in the previous game, a loss to the Lions, that infuriated Fassel. He threatened that if the special teams units did not improve their play immediately, more heads would roll and he would cut four more players every week until they did.

"It was shock. Shock," Fassel said.

The players were terrified. The younger ones, the ones who were primarily on those special teams units, approached veterans like Michael Strahan and Jessie Armstead in the locker room after Fassel's threat.

Those established players knew that Fassel's contract when he was named head coach, negotiated by George Young, gave him full control over the roster during the season. He could only make suggestions for the final roster at the end of the preseason, but once the real games were underway, Fassel could get rid of anyone he wanted to.

The veterans' response to the younger players backed the head coach. "Don't mess with the man," they said. "He's on a mission."

Up next was the unsuspecting media, which Fassel roused from their slumber with the thundering words that had been bouncing around his head since the previous evening.

"If you have the crosshairs, if you have the laser, you can put it right on my chest," he said. "I'll take full responsibility. I'm raising the stakes right now. If this is a poker game, I'm shoving my chips to the middle of the table. I'm raising the ante. Anybody wants in, get in. Anybody wants out, get out, ok? This team is going to the playoffs."

It became instant news. Even in those days just before social media and viral video clips, the world quickly learned about the crazy Giants coach and his bold statement regarding a team that had lost two straight and had been to the postseason just once in the previous six seasons.

"It was the main story on ESPN and everywhere," Fassel chuckled. His son John, now an NFL special teams coordinator with the Rams, was then coaching the Amsterdam Admirals in NFL Europe. "He called my wife and said: 'Is Dad okay?' She said: 'Don't worry about him, he knows what he's doing.'"

At the time, not everyone was so sure. Reporters exchanged confused glances as the media room quivered with a did-that-really-just-happen? vibe upon Fassel's departure from it.

Once he was told about the guarantee, Accorsi recognized he was going to have to fire Fassel if it did not come true.

"If he feels good about the team's chances, that's great," Accorsi practically shrugged to the *New York Times*. "He has the pulse beat of his team."

Some of the players were a bit skeptical, too.

"Jim gets up and he says all those things that he says, pushing my chips to the center of the table, and we're like, 'What the hell are you talking about, coach? We're not that desperate yet,'" Tiki Barber said. "But I think he felt like he was."

Regardless of whether they concurred, everyone understood what Fassel was saying.

"I knew what he meant, putting all his chips into the table and pushing them forward," Jessie Armstead said. "That means you lost, you lost, and all of a sudden you say, 'Hey, there's one hand left and I'm going for the gusto.' To me it was plain and simple. I'm putting everything on the table. You're talking about getting me out of here? Well, you'll get your opportunity because I'm putting everything on the line right now."

"You can't be afraid," Fassel said of the lesson he learned from the guarantee. "You can't coach in the NFL as a head coach afraid for your job. That's the bottom line for me. I put my job on the line. You can't be afraid of that. If you are afraid of that, you shouldn't be a head coach in the NFL. You've gotta have the guts to do it because if you don't have the guts to do it, you're gonna fail. No question about it."

The Giants' next game was against the Cardinals in Arizona on November 26. It would be the first test of Fassel's wager on his team. It did not take long for him to know he had won at least the first hand in his poker game.

The Cardinals won the coin toss and decided to receive. That was fine with Fassel. Before they headed out to midfield, he had directed his captains that he wanted to start the game on defense.

"Kickoff?" they asked, clarifying the directive. "Not defer or receive?"

"Yeah," he said. "We win the toss, we're kicking off."

Eleven players took the field to run under that opening kickoff, knowing that if they didn't do a good enough job, four of them would be gone the following day. They came screaming down the field like a Civil War unit charging a hill, helmets and shoulder pads their bayonets. *Kaboom!*

"The official told me afterward that was the most violent play he'd ever seen in his life," Fassel said. "Everybody wanted to get on it. The referee came over to me and said, 'Jim, what's going on?'"

Fassel knew.

"From then on, we played well on special teams and everywhere else because everyone knew on the offense and defense that if you're not cutting the mustard, I'm cutting you," Fassel said. "They knew I wasn't messing around. If you're not performing, I'm getting rid of you. So everybody picked it up . . . They knew I cared about them. I had a great relationship with the players. But sometimes, everybody does, in the workplace or in football, they don't take things seriously. And when you threaten them…"

They respond. In that first game, they did so with a dominant 31–7 win over the Cardinals to improve to 8–4. The next week it was a 9–7 win over the Redskins, also on the road. The following week, they beat the Steelers, 30–10. That set up a Week 16 game in prime time against the Cowboys at Texas Stadium, when the Giants, at 9–4, had a chance to clinch the NFC East title. The Eagles were 10–5 (they had a bye in Week 16), but the Giants had swept them, so they held a head-to-head tie-breaker.

It should have been a walkover. The Cowboys were 5–9 and had lost much of their star power from their Super Bowl teams of recent years. Michael Irvin retired. Deion Sanders was released. It was Troy Aikman's final season with the Cowboys and Dave Campo's first as their head coach.

Instead, the Cowboys showed fight.

They still had Emmitt Smith, and he ran for a 1-yard touchdown in the first quarter. The Cowboys added a pair of field goals to go ahead, 13–0, at halftime. Had the Giants really come all this way to fall short of fulfilling Fassel's guarantee from a month earlier?

No. In the third quarter, Kerry Collins threw a 33-yard touchdown pass to Amani Toomer to make it 13–7. In the fourth quarter, Emmanuel McDaniel intercepted Aikman to set up a 13-yard touchdown run by Barber to give the Giants a 14–13 lead. After a field goal made it 17–13, Micheal Barrow ended any chances of a Cowboys comeback with a fourth-down tackle of rookie running back Michael Wiley for no gain on fourth-and-2 with 31 seconds left.

The Giants were a playoff team. Just as Fassel had predicted.

"In retrospect it was brilliant," Barber said. "If we have a crappy season and we don't make the playoffs, he's going to get fired. We all know that, and he probably knows it. But, if we respond to it and we go to the postseason, he's brilliant. He predicted this! I don't think he calculated it, but it was a perfect calculation.

"The thing that happened was everybody started talking about how crazy Coach Fassel was and not talking about the things that we were screwing up and the bad things we were doing as players," Barber added. "It took all the pressure off of us. Hell, if our coach is going to go all in, let's get his back. So we went on this run and it was amazing. He gets a lot of credit for it and he deserves a lot of credit for it. He got us right."

Jim Fassel guaranteed the 2000 Giants would make the playoffs. His prediction probably would not have come true if he didn't have the backing of veterans like Michael Strahan and Jessie Armstead. (Newsday Photo by Kathy Kmonicek)

"It was a situation where the team was just about to click," Armstead said. "It happened at the right moment. The right words were said at the right time. And we just let everything hang loose after that. Everything's on the table, you don't have anything to lose. Don't leave no bullets in your gun."

There was, of course, a risk. That's why Fassel used the gambling analogy. He did not know for sure that the Giants would make the playoffs. The young special teams players could have responded to his threats by falling short. The veterans could have thought he was a lame duck grasping at a fraying rope for his job. They could have checked out. *Whatever, dude. Good luck in your next job.*

"We'd be writing the story about how he said that and how the whole season collapsed on him," Armstead said of the alternate history of the 2000 Giants. "It can go either way."

Fassel said he wasn't only challenging the players with his impassioned speeches and vision.

"I had to look at myself," he said. "Maybe I wasn't doing a good enough job, maybe I let them be a little too complacent. I don't know. But when I threatened jobs, it changed the whole dynamic . . . That hurts a lot of coaches today. You're trying to run the Good Ship Lollipop and you can't do that. You can't do that in the NFL. You have to be out there, because then the players will respond to you."

The 2000 Giants did. All the way to the playoffs. All the way to Super Bowl XXXV.

"It worked for me because first I had players who believed in me and second I believed in my players," Fassel said. "They followed what I said. At the end of the day, I think the players respected that."

STRAHAN SETS THE RECORD

Quarterbacks are like home runs: When you're really trying to hit one, that's when it becomes the hardest to do so.

Michael Strahan learned that early in his career. When he came to the Giants, he felt as if he had to keep up with the veterans on the team—Lawrence Taylor in particular—and beef up his stats. He quickly learned, though, that there were more important things to focus on than quarterback sacks.

"I never went into a game and literally said, 'I have to get sacks' like that was the be-all and end-all," the Hall of Fame defensive end said. "Thinking like that doesn't help you."

That's why Strahan always set his mind on being a strong all-around defender.

"People say I was a great pass rusher, but I think I actually played the run better than I rushed the passer," he said. "For me that was actually a bigger joy. I got more joy out of stopping the run than rushing the passer. It's a little more of a macho thing to me. It was more of a physical thing to show that I wasn't one-dimensional. You had to call me a defensive end, you couldn't call me a pass rusher."

For one season, though, Strahan was the best pass rusher there ever was.

In 2001, he set the NFL's single-season record with 22 ½ sacks, terrorizing quarterbacks around the league, dominating offensive linemen to the point of submission, and setting a standard that—to his own surprise—remains to this day.

Through that entire campaign, Strahan spent as little time as possible calculating his pace and doing the math to see how many more he needed to break the sack record that was set by Mark Gastineau of the Jets 17 years earlier.

Until, that is, the end.

In the last game of the season, Strahan finally decided that he wanted it. He went into the game against the Packers on January 6, 2002, at Giants Stadium, an otherwise meaningless contest for a Giants team that would finish 7–9 and out of the playoffs, with one goal in mind.

Head coach Jim Fassel told Strahan that if he got the sack to break the record, he could come out of the game.

"Well, we weren't going anywhere and I was like, 'Ok, you know what? Let me hopefully get it earlier rather than later if I get one at all,'" Strahan said.

Strahan wasn't the only one who was hoping the bleak day would be salvaged by the record-setting performance.

"You love to see your teammate achieve great things," said linebacker Jessie Armstead, a close friend of Strahan's on the team. "A lot of times you see on offense, people get an all-time rushing record or all-time receiving record. For a defense, you don't have too many accolades you can get, and that's one of the biggest ones you can get right there."

The entire Giants defense worked together to get the record for Strahan.

"I'm always coming up acting like I'm aggressive and blitzing and stuff like that," Armstead said. "Maybe I can take one of the blocks off him, maybe take the back trying to chip or something like that. Just different things that we tried to do out there at the end because we wanted to see him get the record. And offenses were trying to do things, too, to prevent him from getting the record."

As the game began, the only real question was whether Strahan would be able to break the record. He had 21 ½ sacks, half a sack shy of the mark.

"I went into that game wanting it, recognizing it, and knowing that everybody wanted me to have it," Strahan said. "But sacks are like anything else, they come and they go. You never know if they'll come in bunches or at all."

It seemed as if this one might pass without any. Into the fourth quarter, Strahan was being shut out. Then, with the Packers comfortably ahead and about three minutes remaining in the game, quarterback Brett Favre called a running play in the huddle with a handoff to Ahman Green. With the offensive line blocking for a run, Favre faked the handoff and kept the ball, ran to his right, and came face-to-face with a practically unblocked Strahan.

There has been plenty written and said about that final sack over the past two decades. Was Favre flopping for his buddy? Did the cheap sack blemish the record?

Michael Strahan's record of 22 1/2 sacks in the 2001 season still stands. But so does controversy over how he achieved it when Brett Favre flopped in front of him. (Newsday LLC/ Paul J. Bereswill)

Strahan wasn't thinking about any of that when he fell on top of Favre.

"Oh my God! He's here and he has the ball in his hands!" Strahan said. He couldn't believe his luck. "At that point, I'm thinking the quarterback is there and I have to get him."

Afterward, things changed. Accusations of a bogus record swirled. It made Strahan wonder if he might have been better off without the record.

"I caught a lot of flak," Strahan said. "People get so caught up. I was like, 'Was it really worth it?' I couldn't care less about that. That wasn't my objective coming into the season, and it wasn't my reason for playing football."

The record he really wanted to break wasn't Gastineau's anyway. It was Taylor's. In 1986, the Giants linebacker had set the franchise mark with 20 ½ sacks. Strahan had broken that one a week earlier against the Eagles.

"That was, to me, the most amazing achievement because this guy was the best to ever play the game in my opinion," Strahan said. "I had the chance to play with him for a year, and I learned so much from him. He's the man. To be able to have a record that he had held before, that was a bigger achievement for me."

Ask Strahan about the record-setting season, and the numbers he thinks about have nothing to do with sacks.

"I think about 9/11," he said.

The Giants opened their season with a 31–20 Monday Night Football loss in Denver on September 10, then flew home to Newark Airport. Their charter landed at around 6 a.m. and pulled up to the terminal. At an adjacent gate, an airplane was idling and waiting for its crew and passengers to board for a cross-country flight to San Francisco. United 93. That flight would never reach its destination, crashing in a field in Pennsylvania after terrorists hijacked it and passengers, aware that other planes in the air had been hijacked and flown into buildings, overtook them.

The world changed that day. The country changed. New York changed.

Everyone was affected. Including Strahan.

"Coming back and experiencing that, going through the rest of the season, it totally switched my mindset," Strahan said.

Eight months earlier, the Giants had played in the Super Bowl. Now they were ambassadors for a city that was trying to simultaneously recover, mourn, heal, remember, move forward, rebuild, grieve, fight, and process the unimaginable.

There were no NFL games played the following weekend. That gave the Giants time to help as much as they could, in any way they could.

They listened to stories about people who would have been at their desk in the World Trade Center had they not been up late the night before watching the game, their lives saved by being a Giants fan in need of a few extra minutes of sleep. They were told how much they meant to those who did perish, how those offices and cubicles were decorated with Giants posters and pennants and ticket stubs and autographed memorabilia. They recognized how important it would be, to those who survived and those who didn't alike, to get back on the field and represent New York with pride and dignity.

They visited firehouses. They appeared with first responders. They went to Ground Zero.

"You saw all these workers, emergency personnel, firefighters, police officers, everybody volunteering," Strahan said. "You saw how tired they were. Completely exhausted. And I said to myself: 'You know what? From here on out I can never complain about being tired, can't say I'm too tired or exhausted to do anything, because this is real. This is what being tired and exhausted is.' And that was a lot more serious than just the game of football. So, from that moment on, I just kind of got myself together. It was like a complete reset on attitude, a complete reset on my career in a lot of different ways."

It's an attitude he still maintains in his new career as an entertainer, crisscrossing the country with a jam-packed schedule that has him hosting a network morning show in New York, a Sunday pregame show in Los Angeles, a number of game shows, and various other appearances and obligations.

At the time, though, Strahan was just a football player. And in the scope of what had happened, that seemed to be the most insignificant thing anyone could be. So, he did the only thing he thought might make the slightest difference to anyone, even himself.

Strahan dedicated his season to those whose lives had been touched by the attacks.

In other words, everyone.

It wasn't much of a season at that point. Strahan didn't have a sack in the opener, didn't have one in the second game in Kansas City (a patriotic victory at Arrowhead Stadium, when it felt as if the entire country were pulling for the New Yorkers). It wasn't until the third game of the season that he recorded his first quarterback takedown against the Saints. He had three in that game.

"After that, I just went on a tear," he said.

He had 1 ½ against Washington, then in the span of three games against the Rams, Eagles, and Redskins, he had a combined 8.

"Of course I heard about it," Strahan said of his ever-climbing total. "It wasn't something that entered my consciousness. Never something I fathomed. So I didn't really pay attention to it. Then eventually people started talking about it."

One and a half against the Cowboys in the eighth game, and he had 14 at the midway point of the season.

In 2001, Michael Strahan had one of the most dominant defensive seasons any player has ever had in NFL history. He set the record with 22 1/2 sacks but always wanted to be recognized as an outstanding all-round player. (Doug Pensinger / Staff, courtesy of Getty Images)

"One thing about those sacks, you can hit a couple of them back-to-back in a couple games and stay hot, and that's what he did," Armstead said. "Things started falling his way. When he got a little past midway through the season, you get that itch and you start smelling it. He just pushed the stone and willed his way to get that record. That's a big-time record, too."

Things began to slow down a bit in the second half of the schedule. He went six straight games without recording more than one sack in any of them, and with two weeks left in the season, he was still at 18. It seemed as if 2001 would be a good season for Strahan, but not a record setter.

"I think a lot of people said, 'Well, it's not really gonna happen,'" Strahan said. "We had two tough opponents coming up, and it was going to be tough."

But on December 30 against the Eagles in Philadelphia, Strahan recorded 3 ½ sacks. It was in that game he broke the franchise record held by Lawrence Taylor.

And it set up the regular-season finale against the Packers with Strahan just a half sack behind Gastineau.

Eventually, the controversy over the Favre sack died down—though it has never quite disappeared—and Strahan has learned to enjoy holding the record. When the 2018 season ended without anyone having reached his number, Strahan set a new record. He's held the single-season sack mark longer than anyone else in NFL history.

Of course, only three men have ever held it at all. Sacks didn't become an official NFL statistic until 1982, and Doug Martin of the Vikings had 11 ½ that season, which, technically, set the record. The following year, Gastineau had 19. Then, in 1984, he had 22. He held the record at that level for 16 seasons before Strahan topped it by a half.

Strahan said he is shocked that his record has stood as long as it has.

"I thought there were a few guys with a great chance to break it, and I really thought they would," he said. "I think eventually it'll happen. The game has changed so much. It's more of a pass-happy league, and so you have a lot more opportunities. And a lot of guys are more specialized at rushing the passer."

That is something Strahan never wanted to be. He wanted to be a more well-rounded player.

Ironically, his 2001 season may have proven him as such more than any other. Armstead called it the most dominant season he has ever seen from a defender.

"You have a guy who had 22 ½ sacks and also was a run stopper," Armstead said. "He didn't let nobody run on him. You see a lot of guys just try to get upfield and do all kinds of things, they're strictly pass rushers."

Not Strahan.

"The sack record is great," Strahan said. "I think everybody else gets a bigger kick out of it than me. Records are meant to be broken, and I'm sure one day it will be broken and I'll be relegated out of the record books."

But never out of the conversation for top defensive seasons of all time, and one of the finest of any kind in Giants history.

GIANTS GET THEIR MANNING

Ernie Accorsi was out hunting quarterbacks. The Giants' general manager had the fourth overall pick in the upcoming 2004 draft, which was chock-full of talent at the most important position in football. The Giants already had a quarterback who had taken them to a Super Bowl in Kerry Collins, but they wanted to land one they could count on to be the face of the franchise for the next decade or longer. That meant Accorsi and the Giants scouts spent most of their Saturdays in late 2003 at college games, breaking down the prospects and coming up with opinions on all of them.

December 18, 2003, found Accorsi in Mobile, Alabama, to watch just such a player. Of course, just about every other decision maker in the NFL was on hand as well, so there was no room in the press box, and Accorsi had to sit outside in the stands. It was miserable. Cold, windy, and damp. "I almost froze to death," Accorsi said.

But the quarterback? He was spectacular. He threw four touchdown passes in the first half. He was on fire. Everyone knew he'd make a great pro and would be a can't-miss player.

Even John Mara, the Giants' president, could tell that while watching the game at home on television. He also knew Accorsi was out shivering in the stands, and he called the general manager at halftime with a message of mercy:

"Come home and warm up," Mara told him. "He's our guy."

The quarterback that day was Ben Roethlisberger, leading Miami of Ohio to a win over Louisville in the GMAC Bowl. When Accorsi left the stadium, the

Giants figured they would be selecting the big-bodied passer in April. They loved everything about him.

Over the coming months, though, something changed. Not so much about their regard for Roethlisberger, but in their appreciation for another quarterback in the draft class. And by the time April 24, 2004, rolled around, and with it the NFL draft, the Giants had a new player in their sights.

Eli Manning.

"We go through the Combine process and all of that and everybody kind of fell in love with Eli," Mara said. "We still loved Roethlisberger, but the difference for us at the time was the level of competition. One guy is in the SEC, the best conference in the country, with not a lot around him, and the other guy was playing at Miami of Ohio. Loved them both. I think the pedigree had something to do with it, too. Here's Peyton dominating the league at the time. We knew he was going to be a solid citizen for us, there was never any worry about that. So, we made the decision that he's the guy."

The problem was, so did the Chargers. And they had the first overall pick in the draft. If the Giants were going to land Manning, they were going to have to trade up with San Diego. And even though the Manning family had made it clear they did not want Eli to play for the Chargers, the team in San Diego had all the leverage.

The night before the draft, Mara was at a function in New York City peppering Accorsi for updates.

"Have you heard from A.J.?" Mara asked several times, referring to A.J. Smith, general manager of the Chargers.

"No," Accorsi told him. "He's gonna take it right down to the wire, but I'm not going to give in on this."

There were about seven minutes left on the clock before the Giants' selection, and they had all but given up. They had a deal in place with the Browns to move down to the sixth overall selection, acquire a few extra picks in the process, and land Roethlisberger there. It was all set.

Then Accorsi's phone rang. It was Smith proposing a trade.

The Chargers had already selected Manning, but they would give him to the

Giants in exchange for a package of draft picks plus defensive end Osi Umenyiora. Accorsi said no.

Smith made a counteroffer. He suggested they could work out a trade if the Giants picked Philip Rivers with their fourth pick. The danger for the Giants would be taking Rivers and then having a deal fall through and being stuck with the third quarterback on their wish list.

"Ernie and A.J. are playing a game of chicken," Mara said. "Neither one wants to tip their hand about it. But Ernie was determined that we were going to get Eli."

The Giants agreed.

"I took a risk," Accorsi said. "If he would have called back and said I'm backing out of this trade, there's no Ben for me."

As it turned out, Accorsi wound up with the quarterback he began the day coveting. The Giants traded Rivers, their third-round pick in 2004, and their first- and fifth-round picks in the 2005 draft to the Chargers for Manning.

The final sticking point in the negotiations was the least valuable piece of the puzzle: that 2005 fifth-rounder. The Chargers had thrown it into their list of demands just before an agreement was reached, and it nearly scuttled the whole deal.

"My initial reaction was: 'They're gonna make the deal, they're bluffing on that,'" John Mara said. "'They'll still make the deal. We don't have to give them that.'"

Mara's brother, Frank, who was in the war room during those negotiations, spoke up.

"Do you really want to lose this guy over a fifth-round pick?" Frank asked.

The answer was no. The Maras gave Accorsi the approval to make the deal.

Frank Mara may have convinced John Mara to complete the trade for Manning, but John Mara had to convince Wellington Mara.

"My father initially was against doing the deal," John Mara said. "He was still a big Kerry Collins fan. I think he also was feeling his age a little bit, asking himself: 'Are we going to start all over with a new quarterback? We've got a pretty good team right now.'"

There were plenty of big-time players in the 2004 draft besides quarterbacks who could have helped the Giants immediately. The class is always remembered for the three passers, but that first round also produced Larry Fitzgerald, Sean Taylor, Kellen Winslow Jr., Jonathan Vilma, Vince Wilfork, and Benjamin Watson. Wellington thought the Giants should be exploring those players, not just quarterbacks.

"So we had to work on him a little bit," Mara said.

Accorsi would call John Mara that spring, urging the son to talk to his father and convince him of the benefits of picking a quarterback.

"I remember I kept telling him that if this guy truly is a franchise quarterback, which we believe he will be, we will be in a position where we can win championships and be competitive as long as he plays," Mara said. "Once you have a franchise quarterback, everything falls into place."

Wellington Mara eventually gave in, but he was not happy about it initially. And when he saw Manning perform so poorly at his first practice in rookie mini-camp a few weeks after the draft, a display so ghastly and erratic that the quarterback was throwing passes cockeyed and hitting tackling dummies on the sideline instead of receiving targets, he probably was even less happy.

But soon, he was completely on board.

Giants coowner Wellington Mara had to be convinced that adding Eli Manning was the right move. Here, he meets his new quarterback shortly after the Giants traded for him on draft day. (Copyright © New York Football Giants, Inc.)

"He fell in love with Eli pretty quickly, but he was not happy about it at first," Mara said. "He knew that once we took him, Kerry would probably have to go. But he gave his ok, Ernie completes the deal, and I remember feeling the elation."

So once the trade was finalized, who was the first to tell Eli Manning he'd become a Giant?

An 11-year-old kid named Dylan Sherwyn.

He was backstage at the 2004 NFL Draft at Madison Square Garden—a friend of his father's had been able to get them passes—and happened to be in the room where the grim-faced Manning, clad in light blue and lightning bolts, was being interviewed by reporters. But Sherwyn also had an eye on a television set in the corner that was covering the rest of the draft. That's when he saw Commissioner Paul Tagliabue step to the microphone and announce the trade between the Chargers and the Giants.

"Dad," Sherwyn said, "he's still wearing his Chargers stuff. He's wearing the wrong team. Should I tell him he got traded?"

The answer: "Go for it."

So he did.

"Some kid kind of busted through the door yelling, 'Manning's been traded to the Giants!'" is how Manning remembered it. Though it may not have been that dramatic, it certainly felt that way for the quarterback. "I thought he might be joking."

Manning remembers turning to the NFL official who was escorting him through the media interviews. He was wearing an earpiece. Manning looked at him with an is-this-kid-messing-with-me? expression on his face.

"He looked kind of stunned," Sherwyn said of Manning.

Sherwyn couldn't stick around very long. In a matter of seconds, an army of cameras and reporters converged on the newest quarterback for the New York Giants. The Chargers cap Manning had been wearing flew off the top of his head and was quickly replaced by one with an NY logo.

The two did meet up again soon enough. Manning and the Giants invited the Sherwyns—Jets fans from New Jersey, by the way—to the Giants-Jets preseason game that August. After the game, Dylan and his family were escorted to the

Giants' locker room, where they met with Manning. The rookie quarterback had an awful night, getting picked on by the Jets defense and essentially proving to the Giants and the world that he was not ready to be the starter in Week 1. That job went to Kurt Warner. Still, Manning posed for photos and signed autographs, including one on a copy of the *New York Times* article that initially chronicled their draft day interaction.

He'd become a Giant. Now the team had to figure out how to make Manning their starting quarterback.

They began the season with Warner at the position, with Manning getting some on-field experience at the end of the first two games. They were 5–4, having just returned home from a loss to the Cardinals in Arizona, when Tom Coughlin made what would become the last quarterback decision he ever faced with the Giants. On November 15, 2004, it was announced that Manning was going to be the starter.

When the Giants acquired Eli Manning in 2004, they did not know it would bring them a decade and a half of quarterback stability... as well as two Super Bowls. (Harry How / Staff, courtesy of Getty Images)

"Coach Coughlin just told me that it was what he felt was best for the organization moving forward," Warner said of the demotion. "Basically told me, 'This has nothing to do with you, it has nothing to do with your play and what you haven't done.' What I believe he was trying to say was, I think we all understood that even though we had a decent record, we weren't a great football team. To go down that path with me was just kind of prolonging the inevitable."

Coughlin thought the change could give the Giants a spark. Instead, it sunk their season.

"I remember being excited because of the pedigree of the young man and what he could become," running back Tiki Barber recalled of the switch. "But then the struggles immediately following, those six games were torturous. Just mistake after mistake… It was frustrating seeing a quarterback like Kurt who had had some success, had won a Super Bowl, get pulled for the young kid and having no idea where it was going to go."

It wasn't as inevitable as it should have been looking back that Manning would be given a chance in 2004. Although the Giants had paid the high premium for the young quarterback in the trade, had they not stumbled in those two games against the Bears and Cardinals after their 4–2 start, things could have turned out differently.

"If we had won those games or maybe even won one of them, that would have delayed Eli's appearance, I think," Mara said.

In his book *A Team to Believe In*, which was written after the 2007 Super Bowl season, Coughlin wrote about the decision. He noted that the media "crushed" him for giving up on a potential playoff season but that Wellington Mara, when told by Coughlin he was going to make the move to Manning, smiled and told him: "We think the same way."

Not everyone did. And this time it was John Mara's turn to need convincing.

"I remember being a little concerned about it at the time because Kurt Warner had played fairly well for us," John Mara said. "Because he struggled for most of the second half of the season, I remember questioning whether that was the right move or not because we had a chance to have a decent year that year."

The Giants dropped six straight by some overwhelming scores. They lost, 14–10, to the Falcons and Michael Vick at Giants Stadium on November 21, 2004, then fell to the Eagles, 27–6, and to the Redskins, 31–7. The low point was the 37–14 loss at Baltimore in which Manning completed 4 of 18 passes, threw two interceptions, and had a passer rating of 0.0.

"I think you always feel like you're ready and then you play and you learn and you realize it's hard to prepare for everything," Manning said. "You learn so much from just playing in games, from mistakes or different looks from defenses. You always feel like you are prepared and ready to go. You always learn a lot along the way."

The Giants stuck with him, though. He played well in a 33–30 loss to the Steelers in December, facing off against almost-Giant Ben Roethlisberger for the first time. And in the final game of the year, Manning engineered a game-winning drive to beat the Cowboys, 28–24, for his first win as a starter.

"The last game my father ever saw was the final game of the 2004 season against Dallas when Eli takes us up the field at the end of the game and wins the game for us," John Mara said. "That was the last game he was ever at."

Before he died, Wellington Mara had glimpsed the future.

Manning started 210 consecutive regular-season games for the Giants, the second-longest streak in NFL history at the time it ended when he was benched for Geno Smith in a Week 12 game against the Raiders in 2017 (Head Coach Ben McAdoo and General Manager Jerry Reese, who had engineered the lineup move, were fired the following day). He won two Super Bowls for the Giants. He set every passing record in Giants history and played more games in a Giants uniform than anyone else ever had.

"That separates the teams that have success and the teams that don't have success, having a franchise quarterback that plays every week and plays at a high level," Mara said. "Even when the rest of your team isn't so good, you always have a chance to win. It lifts the whole franchise when you have a quarterback who can play at that level."

Just hours before Manning earned his first win, Mara was on the field for pregame warm-ups chatting with former Giants coach Bill Parcells, then the head coach for Dallas. Mara asked Parcells how he was doing.

"Not as good as you," Parcells said.

"What do you mean?" Mara asked aghast. "We're in last place!"

"Yeah," Parcells said, "but you have a quarterback."

FOR THE DUKE

Hey, are you gonna keep getting caught or are you gonna score a touchdown?

That was the question posed to Tiki Barber as he came to the sideline huffing and puffing after his second long run against the Redskins that did not find the end zone. He'd opened the game on October 30, 2005, with a dash of 57 yards around the left side and then peeled off a 59-yarder in the second quarter, only to be stopped at the 1. Brandon Jacobs ran it in from there on the next play.

Barber was having one of the greatest games of his career, the Giants were cruising, but there was one glaring omission. No touchdown.

The person who posed the blunt but playful question to Barber wasn't a coach or even a teammate. It was Tim McDonnell, one of the grandchildren of Giants owner Wellington Mara. McDonnell and Barber had been friendly for years going back to when McDonnell was a young ball boy during training camps. When Barber was a rookie in 1997, it was McDonnell who took care of Barber's locker at SUNY Albany and ran errands for the running back. They'd stayed in touch through the years despite spending less time together. Barber even attended McDonnell's graduation party when he matriculated from Holy Cross and was about to begin a job with the football program at Notre Dame. Now McDonnell was a 22-year-old and on the sideline of this game at Giants Stadium giving guff to the best running back in team history.

"Timmy," Barber said, "I promise you, before this day is over, I am going to score you a touchdown. And I'm going to bring you the ball."

It was a game the Giants knew they'd have to play all season, they just didn't know when. Wellington Mara, their long-time Hall of Fame coowner, was dying of lymphoma, and Head Coach Tom Coughlin began the year by telling the players that they were going to be "the team of record" for Mara and coowner Robert Tisch (who was battling brain cancer at the same time). Everyone knew there was a good chance neither of the men would live to see the end of the season.

By late October, it became clear that Mara was fading quickly. The Giants beat the Broncos, 24–23, on October 23, knowing it was likely to be the final game of Mara's life.

That Tuesday, Barber received a call from the team's long-time trainer Ronnie Barnes, summoning him to the Mara family home in Westchester to say his good-byes to Wellington. He quickly drove up from his place in Manhattan.

"I walked in, and it was such a somber feeling in the house," Barber recalled. "I passed on my thoughts and prayers (to the family members). And before I left I got a chance to go sit with him, Mr. Mara."

He was sleeping.

"I remember just looking at him and holding his hand and thanking him for being a part of bringing me to New York and letting me be a Giant. And then I left."

Mara died later that night at age 89.

The rest of the week was a whirlwind of emotion as the Giants dealt with the loss of their beloved owner while also trying to prepare for the Redskins. On Friday, Mara's funeral took place at St. Patrick's Cathedral in New York City. The building was crammed with a who's who of luminaries from the worlds of sports and business and popular culture. The team was bused to Manhattan for the service and listened to a stirring eulogy from Wellington's oldest son, John, who had already assumed the role of team president several years earlier.

It was a gloomy, overcast gray day with a high ceiling of clouds, not atypical of autumn in New York. "The perfect day for a funeral," Barber said.

The Giants then boarded the buses and returned to New Jersey for their practice. While they were stretching, just as Coughlin walked past Barber, those dreary clouds parted just enough to allow a stream of sunshine to reach the field.

"Coach," Barber said to Coughlin, "that's Wellington looking down on us."

Coughlin gazed up at the sky.

"Yeah," he said. "You're probably right."

Wellington Mara was a fixture on the sideline during Giants practices and games, and his legacy lives on with his nickname imprinted on every football the NFL uses. (Copyright © New York Football Giants, Inc.)

Wellington Mara was one of the most influential figures in American sports. Named after the Duke of Wellington by his father, Giants founder Tim Mara, he was born in Rochester, New York, on August 14, 1916. He was a nine-year-old ball boy for the Giants during their inaugural season in 1925 but quickly climbed the ranks. How quickly? In 1930, five years later, Tim Mara split his ownership interest between sons, 14-year-old Wellington and his brother Jack. Wellington was the Boy King of the Giants. The Tutankhamun of his day.

After he graduated from Fordham, Wellington came to work for the Giants' front office as treasurer and assistant to his father. In 1940, he became the team's secretary. After serving in World War II, he returned to be named the team's vice-president. When his uncle died in 1965, seven years after his grandfather had passed, Wellington became president of the Giants.

He played not just a huge role with the Giants, helping to assemble the teams that would exemplify the franchise's glory in the 1950s and early '60s with Frank Gifford, Sam Huff, Roosevelt Brown and Y.A. Tittle, but was instrumental in much of the framework that today makes the NFL one of the world's most prosperous sports leagues. In an age when the Giants were the NFL's biggest draw, it was Mara who championed the idea of revenue sharing from television contracts so that teams in bigger markets would not have a financial advantage over those from smaller outposts. It was a concept that probably hurt the Giants but allowed the NFL to thrive.

Wellington Mara's memory lives on in every NFL contest. Since 1941, when Wilson became the official manufacturer of gameday balls for the league, every game has been played with the same model. Since Tim Mara played such a large role in striking the deal with Wilson, legendary Bears owner and coach George Halas thought that the model should be named "The Duke" as a way of honoring the Mara family. To this day, every official NFL football is imprinted with that nickname: "The Duke."

The game that followed his passing was a blowout. There was no team that could have stood between the Giants and a victory in that game and thwarted their efforts to revere their beloved owner. The afternoon at Giants Stadium began with his granddaughter, Kate Mara, not yet the well-known actress she would eventually become, singing the national anthem. Fans brought signs thanking and honoring Wellington where once he had been hung in effigy from the upper deck.

The service on Friday at St. Patrick's had been for family and dignitaries. This game was for the fans to say their good-byes.

And it started out about as perfectly as possible. Barber took that first toss to the left, and it was blocked perfectly, as if the players themselves were the X's and O's on the paper when the play was drawn up. More such plays continued. Barber snapped off the 59-yarder to the 1. The Giants defense was throttling the Redskins just as badly. By halftime, the Giants led, 19–0. Jeremy Shockey, the only other active Giant beside Barber who was asked to visit Wellington's bedside in his final days, caught a 10-yard touchdown pass from Eli Manning to open the second half. By late in the third quarter, it was 29–0, and soon, after Osi Umenyiora recovered a fumble at the Washington 23, the Giants were once again on the doorstep of the end zone.

The only thing missing from making it a perfect day was a touchdown by Barber.

When the Giants reached first-and-goal from the 6, that's when the effort to get Barber into the scoring column ramped up. He took a handoff to the left for 2 yards, then a handoff right for no gain. On third-and-goal from the 4, Barber took the ball up the middle on a draw play. All-Pro safety Sean Taylor came flying in to attempt a tackle, but Barber managed to dive over him and stretched the ball over the goal line.

Barber left the ball on the turf and blew a kiss into the air, just as he normally did after touchdowns. Then he quickly realized that this was not a normal touchdown. He went back and picked the football off the turf and carried it to the sideline as a keepsake.

But not for himself.

He immediately flipped the ball to McDonnell, the grandson of Wellington Mara, his former personal valet, who had goaded him earlier about getting caught from behind on the two long runs.

"Timmy," Barber said, "this is for you and your family and the Duke for making me a Giant. Thank you, guys. I love you all."

At the end of an emotional week, McDonnell said he didn't know whether to smile or cry.

"It was everything coming together at once," he said. "It was special. Really special."

McDonnell is now a pro scout for the Giants. His office at the team's facility in New Jersey, like most others in the building, is decorated with plenty of Giants regalia and a few game balls from memorable contests. Most of them are painted and written on to tell their story from various victories. But in a glass case in his office sits an unadorned football. It's the one that Barber tossed to him during that game.

"Just the way it was that day," McDonnell said.

The only way anyone would know its significance without asking would be to look at the sideline credential from that game, which is also in the case.

Like every NFL football since 1941, this one boasts its model name, too. Yet somehow, "The Duke" seems to stand out more on this one than the others.

After the touchdown, Barber was through. There was still another quarter left in the game, but he'd done what he set out to do. Like a sculptor who must know when to put down his chisel or a painter who needs to recognize when to lay down his brush, he'd finished his masterpiece. He had the touchdown. He'd run for 206 yards on 24 carries through three quarters and said he could have probably run for 300 if he'd stayed on the field.

"But I didn't want to," he said. "It was unnecessary. I don't need to add anymore."

That decision would prove to play a role in determining the NFL's rushing leader when the season ended. Barber had his best year as a pro. He took to heart Coughlin's preseason challenge about being the "team of record" for the two owners. He finished with 2,390 all-purpose yards, the second-most at the time in NFL history behind Marshall Faulk, and after he ran for 203 in the regular-season finale against the Raiders in Oakland, he had a league-leading 1,860 rushing yards. That was 53 more yards that Seattle's Shaun Alexander had.

Alexander had planned to sit out his team's final game that season. The Seahawks were heading to the playoffs—eventually to the Super Bowl—and he thought he had the rushing crown locked up. Then he saw Barber's performance earlier in the day, did some quick math, and changed his mind.

Tiki Barber called his performance against the Redskins in the game immediately following the death of beloved coowner Wellington Mara "my forever Giants moment." (Tom Berg / Staff, courtesy of Getty Images)

"He told me, 'I saw you rushed for 203 yards and I wasn't supposed to play, but I was like, fuck that, I'm playing!'" Barber said. Alexander took 20 carries in a meaningless game against the Packers and ran for 73 yards to finish his season with 1,880. Twenty more than Barber.

"I always tell people: 'If I would have not taken myself out in that Redskins game, I would have had the rushing title that year,'" Barber said. "But that wasn't important to me. It was more important to do what I had to do to pay my respects to one of the great men that I ever met."

That Redskins game may feel like an unfinished symphony to some, but to Barber it was complete.

"I did what I set out to do, which was have my greatest day as a Giant," he said. "That was my forever Giant moment."

FROZEN

For a few moments, the visiting locker room at Lambeau Field was empty but for one solitary person. Lawrence Tynes sat on the stool in front of his station in the corner of the room, trying to shake off the cold and absorb what had just happened.

Was it real? Had he actually just kicked a 47-yard field goal to win the NFC Championship in overtime? Had he run onto the field on fourth down and dared his head coach to use him after missing two straight attempts, including an ugly one on the final play of regulation that he considered the worst kick of his career? Were the Giants really going to the Super Bowl?

And the biggest question of all: where the hell is everybody?

Tynes had become a postseason legend and a franchise hero, and there was no one to share it with except for the eerily silent lockers that filled the room. He'd made his kick and bolted off the field, through the tunnel, up the stairs, down the hallway, up another set of stairs. Was the game still going on? Was there a penalty? Had the kick of his life been overturned?

"I'm at my locker just kind of going, 'What the hell just happened?'" Tynes said.

Then, finally, some of the offensive linemen barreled boisterously into the room. Starting guard Rich Seubert was the first one Tynes saw. That's when he knew it was real, that it had actually happened, and it wasn't some hypothermic-induced hallucination.

The rest of the team quickly followed the linemen into the cramped space at the oldest stadium in the NFL.

"And then," Tynes said, "we just kind of celebrated."

The coldest game in Giants franchise history wound up being one of the most thrilling, as well. On January 20, 2008, the Giants faced the Packers at Lambeau Field in the NFC Championship Game with a temperature at kickoff of minus-1 degrees. That, coupled with 12-mile-per-hour winds, made it feel like minus-23. It was the third-coldest game in NFL history.

The Giants knew they'd be facing such elements. All week, they brainstormed not only a game plan to beat the Packers, but one to handle the bone-cracking cold that was forecast for the day of the contest. There were all kinds of ideas floated about which cleats to wear and which gloves to employ. As for staying warm, the Giants were up for just about anything.

The night before the game, the team stayed in Appleton, Wisconsin, about a 30-minute drive from Green Bay. It's the same small town where the Cowboys had stayed when they played in the famous Ice Bowl in 1967. The players thought it might be a good idea to acclimate themselves to the cold, so they spent time that night outdoors.

"We walked back and forth to the restaurants in the area," Brandon Jacobs said before chuckling over the small town that Appleton is. "Actually, there was only one."

On the day of the game, the Giants boarded their bus and headed for Lambeau. They drove up Interstate 41, staring at all those motionless snow-covered dairy farms, the condensation on the inside of the windows freezing into crystals that could be scraped off and pinched together into miniature snowballs.

"You realized it was different," Tynes said.

When the Giants arrived at Lambeau, they tried everything they could to go through their normal routines. It just wasn't possible. It was too cold to function. Jacobs said he spent just a minute or two on the field during what turned out to be misnamed warm-ups. He'd normally catch 25–30 passes from third-string quarterback Jared Lorenzen. On that day, he caught five and ducked back inside. Tynes could barely practice his kicks. Instead of trying a dozen or so from each end of the field, he managed just four and only on one end. His holder, the punter Jeff Feagles, couldn't even catch the snaps and set them down for him. It did not bode well.

"No matter how fast we ran, how hard we did things out there, we were freezing," Jacobs said. "We couldn't stay out there long."

Just prior to the game, the Giants players were slathering a warming gel on one another's bare chests and backs. It was supposed to allow them to maintain warmth in their core and provide an extra layer of protection. Like sunblock, but the opposite.

"None of that stuff worked," Jacobs said.

Eventually, it came time to leave the relative warmth of the locker room and head out onto the field for what was for so many of the Giants the biggest game of their lives.

"I was saying: 'It's cold, but we have to suck it up and go get it,'" Jacobs recalled. "At the end of the day, we just went out there and said, 'Hey, if we win this game, we'll be playing in 80-degree weather in Arizona. This is a three-hour game, max.' I can do anything for three hours."

It wound up taking a little longer than that.

Tom Coughlin was a man of routine, but in such frigid conditions, even he had to make concessions. As he dressed in the coaches' locker room at Lambeau Field before the game, he put on the layers and layers of thermals and sweatshirts that the equipment staff had laid out for him. He slid his hands into big bulky gloves and felt inside of them for the heating elements that would try to keep him warm. He tucked similar pouches of warmth into his shoes to keep his feet as toasty as possible, too.

But when it was time head out onto the field, Coughlin instinctively reached for the same piece of clothing he had been wearing all season and throughout the playoff run. His baseball cap.

"Bad idea," he wrote in his book, *A Team to Believe In*. "Within a minute I can feel my ears begin to freeze. The top of my ears feel like they are going to break off."

More than that, his face was turning bright red. Even when he switched from the baseball cap to a ski hat to cover his ears, Coughlin's ruddy cheeks had no protection, and they began to glow like radioactive tomatoes. Players saw it and grew concerned for his well-being. Everyone watching the game on television saw it, too, as the cameras zoomed in on Coughlin's colorful countenance every chance they got. Up in a warm suite, Coughlin's wife, Judy, was fielding calls and text messages from family and friends begging her to run down and give her husband a scarf or a ski mask or some other protection.

"I was really concerned with the way he was looking," Brandon Jacobs said. "We didn't know whether or not he was going to end up having frostbite or go to the hospital. We didn't want him to be hurt under any situation, so a lot of us were really concerned about him."

At halftime, the team went into the locker room, and that brought the redness down.

"But when we went back out it came right back," Jacobs said. "He probably did get frostbit. I was like, 'Really? This dude's face is like this?'"

It would become one of the most iconic images of that Giants' season. Coughlin, letting nothing stand in his way, not even the penetrating cold that was clearly causing some level of physical damage or the concerns of his players and family and friends for his well-being. Like a sea captain staring down a ferocious wind, Coughlin refused to alter his course to the demands of nature or anything else.

Yet no one had said anything to Coughlin about it. There he was, making this statement with his face simultaneously frozen and ablaze, and he had no idea it was happening. He was just coaching.

It wasn't until after the game that Coughlin knew what the cold had done to his cheeks.

Most people remember the end of the game when they think of that NFC Championship. Most Giants remember the beginning. The Packers received the ball first, gained two quick first downs, and then punted. The Giants offense took the field at their own 18. That's when Jacobs, the Giants' 6-foot-4, 265-pound running back, declared his team's intention to not be intimidated by either the Packers or their home-field weather advantage.

He may have been too cold to stay outside during warm-ups, but when the game began, Jacobs brought the heat.

The first snap of the game for the offense went to Jacobs running right, and he trucked All-Pro safety and future Hall of Famer Charles Woodson, burying his helmet under Woodson's chin and sending him flying backward for a 5-yard gain.

"When he hit him, I felt bad," fellow Giants running back Ahmad Bradshaw said. "I've always been a Woodson fan, but when Brandon Jacobs hits anybody, it's like a man against a boy."

Giants linebacker Antonio Pierce would call it "the biggest play of our entire playoff run."

It was a declaration of the indominable spirit that the 2007 Giants personified. But it wasn't meant to be. At least not by Jacobs.

He knew that the Giants would have to throw the ball to beat the Packers. So, as he was running with the ball, he had a choice to make. He could follow the flow of his offensive linemen to the sideline and probably pick up five or six yards. Or he could do what he wound up doing.

"I ran smack into [Woodson]," Jacobs said. "I figured if I could daze him and have him woozy for the rest of the game, then we could pick on him and get some free yardage with Amani Toomer and Plaxico Burress. We could hit some big plays on him."

It helped. Eli Manning threw the ball 40 times, completing 21 of them, for 251 yards. Burress, shadowed by cornerback Al Harris most of the day, caught 11 of those passes for 151 yards. Jacobs, though, wasn't satisfied.

"I felt like we should have taken a little bit more advantage of Woodson because he was out on his feet the whole first half," Jacobs said. "At the time I thought if I can daze him and take him out of his game, one of the better players in the league, if we can take him away from the game plan, we have a better chance of winning."

Whatever his motivations, whatever the effect, Jacobs's run ignited the Giants.

"I really wanted to smack him," Jacobs said. "I was hoping I stayed up because he had no more outside containment. If I had run him over and [kept my feet] and could have gotten 15–20 more yards and hit that sideline, that play would have been even more special."

On such a frigid day, it must have been painful not just for Woodson to absorb that hit, but for Jacobs to deliver it, no?

"I didn't feel anything," Jacobs said. "I was built for games like that."

The Giants wound up taking a 3–0 lead on that opening drive and were ahead, 6–0, after Tynes kicked his second field goal. Bradshaw and Jacobs each ran for a touchdown, and the Giants' defense held the Packers to 28 rushing yards and just one third-down conversion on 10 tries. Early in the fourth quarter, though, the Packers kicked a field goal to tie the score at 20 after R.W. McQuarters intercepted a pass by Brett Favre but fumbled it on the return to give Green Bay good field position.

The game would come down to a field goal attempt by Tynes. Or, it turned out, several attempts.

The first try was from 43 yards with 6:49 left in the game.

"I hit it really well, I really did, and it went left," Tynes said. "Ho hum. I knew there was only seven minutes left in the game, but I didn't think much of it. That was kind of my mind-set my whole career. I just hoped I'd get another chance. I didn't really harp on misses too much. I hit it really well, it was just a little left. So I said, 'Well, next time I go out here I'm going to aim a little bit farther right.'"

The next time came at the end of regulation. The Giants drove the ball to the 18, Manning spiked it to stop the clock with four seconds left, and Tynes went out confident that his 36-yard attempt would win the game.

"I'm like, 'Ok, we're winning this, not a problem,'" Tynes said. "And I get out there, and it was one of the worst kicks I've ever had. That was one of the worst kicks I ever put my foot on. I was trying to buy time by leaning backward and leaning a little bit left."

The ball knuckled wide and never came close to the uprights. The game was going to overtime. Sudden-death overtime. And the Packers won the coin toss to get the ball first.

Brett Favre. Lambeau Field. The Frozen Tundra. All of it was about to come crashing down on the Giants' dreams.

But on the second snap of the overtime, Corey Webster intercepted a pass by Favre to give the Giants the ball back at the Packers' 34. They were already in field goal range.

"Webby comes over to me and says, 'Alright, I got you another one,'" Tynes said. "That was kind of cool."

The players had confidence in Tynes. The coaches? Not so much.

The Giants ran three plays, the third of them an incompletion to Steve Smith, and offensive coaches Kevin Gilbride and Mike Sullivan were on the headsets pleading with Coughlin to go for it on fourth-and-5 and not put the team's fate on the frozen foot of a kicker who had just muffed their chance to win the game at the end of regulation.

Tynes, though, didn't even wait for the decision to be made. He made it for Coughlin.

"As soon as that ball hit the ground [on third down], I bolted out, zoom," Tynes said. "I was way out, found my spot, and I'm looking around and I don't see Jeff and I don't see any of the field goal unit. I'm just kind of like, 'uhhh...' And then, sure enough, I see Jeff and Coughlin kind of conferencing a little bit and he sent Jeff out there. And we made the kick. The rest is history."

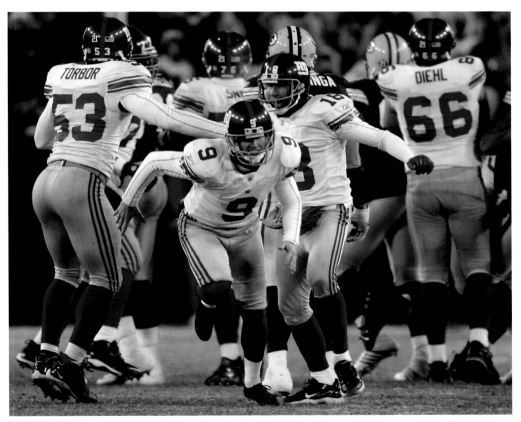

After he kicked the game-winning field goal at frigid Lambeau Field to send the Giants to Super Bowl XLII, Lawrence Tynes sprinted off the field just to get warm. (Jed Jacobsohn / Staff, courtesy of Getty Images)

A 47-yard game-winner just 2:35 into overtime for a 23–20 victory.

"I hit that one as good as I hit the 43-yarder, but I just started it on the right path to begin with," Tynes said. "I started it right at the right upright, and it curled in. Even though that miss was bad with seven minutes left, I learned from it. I was 3-for-5 that day, and it was still the best day I ever had in my life."

Tynes didn't stick around to enjoy the moment on the field. He sprinted straight to the locker room.

"I really just wanted to get the hell out of the cold," he said. "I was so done with all of it."

The rest of the team soon followed. In the mayhem and exultation of that scene, Tynes eventually removed his cleats. Because he had worn his shoes so tight and had on a sock that compressed his foot, he didn't realize the damage that was being done by slamming it into a frozen football over and over again throughout the game. When he took those restrictions off, a nasty welt the size of a baseball popped up. He had broken so many blood vessels in his foot that there was consideration he might not be able to fly home with the team. He didn't kick a football for another 11 days, not until the Thursday before the Super Bowl when the team was in Arizona. He had it drained, but his foot was black and bruised and swollen and looked like it was dead.

There were a few days when it was questionable whether Tynes would even be able to play in the next game.

"I'm glad there are two weeks between the Championship Game and the Super Bowl," Tynes said. "I would have figured out a way, I guess, to play. But every kick I had in the Super Bowl hurt like frigging hell."

And for the rest of his career, Tynes would carry that pain in his right foot. Every time he played in even chilly conditions, he would feel the ache from that day. If he mishit a ball even by fractions of an inch up his foot, it would throb.

It's become like a little memento of the game, of that day, of that whole experience, frozen inside his body.

"When you're in the moment and playing in it, it seems like you just have to do it," Tynes said. "But at 40 years old right now thinking about playing in that? I just don't know how we did it. I don't know how any of us did it."

THE CATCH

At first, David Tyree did not know what all the fuss was about. As he conducted interviews in the depths of University of Phoenix Stadium after Super Bowl XLII, he couldn't really grasp why everyone wanted to talk to him. The Giants had beaten the Patriots, and Tyree had caught a touchdown and another pass as part of the game-winning drive. But there were so many stars on the team—Eli Manning and Plaxico Burress, who connected on the game-winning touchdown; Michael Strahan and Osi Umenyiora and Justin Tuck, who had kept Tom Brady off-balance all game—that he could not comprehend why everyone wanted to talk to him, a player hardly anyone had heard of just a few hours earlier.

It was Tyree's first introduction to his new life. That of Super Bowl icon.

Perhaps in the history of Giants football there had never been a more unlikely player to be thrust into such a stratosphere of celebrity, to become so identified with a singular moment on the field. When Tyree jumped straight up in the air, held the football against his blue Giants helmet, withstood a hit from one of the NFL's fiercest defenders, and came to the ground with it between his red gloves, he put a visual stamp on the sport like few others in the history of football have ever managed.

This book is about Miracle Moments, and in most cases, that adjective is admittedly stretched a bit thin. There have been decisions and plays and games that altered the course of the Giants' history, and football's history, but most of them were orchestrated by mortals. Tyree's remarkable catch, however, seems to rise above the others the same way he rose above the turf in Phoenix on that Super Bowl Sunday evening and came back down to earth with a football pinned up against his head. There is a certain divinity to it. An otherworldliness. Something that defies logic and reason.

If ever there was a Miracle Moment for the Giants, it was this.

But at the time, the magnitude of it had yet to hit him. There was still a game to win. The Giants trailed with 59 second left when Tyree stood up off the grass, and they needed another 24 yards to go to reach the end zone. They wound up beating the Patriots, 17–14, and Tyree was the one standing behind Eli Manning when he took the final knee to end the game, the first to embrace the Super Bowl-winning quarterback. All of that was going through his head—along with the memory of his mother, Thelma, who had died of a heart attack at age 59 just over a month earlier—when reporters began peppering Tyree with questions on February 3, 2008.

Even then, the enormity of it all escaped him.

"I knew it was a great catch," Tyree says of his helmet grab. "Historic? No. It was pretty wild. I didn't see it until I got back to the hotel, so I didn't realize it was that big of a deal. My immediate interviews were giving Eli all the credit. That was half the miracle right there. But I had no claims to any greatness other than the fact that it was a good catch."

It was only later that he began to comprehend its place in Giants history and NFL lore when one of the founders of NFL Films gave it his stamp of approval.

"Once I saw Steve Sabol's quote, I knew I was on to something," Tyree said. "I didn't know much about NFL history, but I knew Steve Sabol did. Once he said that this was the greatest play in Super Bowl history, I just kind of rolled with him and let everybody else do the speaking. Obviously, there were a lot of interviews, and I expected that, but once he said that, I realized this was something way beyond me."

There is The Catch. And there is all that led up to The Catch. The actual act of securing the football was only the final act in a play that began many years earlier for David Tyree.

Growing up in Montclair, New Jersey, just seven miles from Giants Stadium, he was a standout high school athlete whose abilities were being weighed down by drugs and alcohol. Every weekend, he said, he would drink a 40-ounce bottle of malt liquor, a half-pint of Jack Daniels, and smoke marijuana. Those habits stayed

Some plays help win championships, others become iconic moments in sports history. David Tyree's catch against the Patriots in Super Bowl XLII was both. (Nick Laham / Staff, courtesy of Getty Images)

with him through his playing career at Syracuse, where he often drank until he blacked out, and into the NFL with the Giants. Teammate Amani Toomer recalls Tyree showing up for practices smelling of liquor as a rookie in 2003, and he was chronically late for meetings and other team functions.

The Giants fined him repeatedly, and to make up for the lost income, he turned to selling marijuana.

In March 2004, he was arrested when police found half a pound of pot in his car during a traffic stop as he was coming off the George Washington Bridge into Fort Lee, New Jersey.

The charges were eventually dropped, and the Giants stuck with Tyree, who began to turn his life around. He became a man of faith, a solid citizen, a stronger father, and a better teammate. He was still mostly a special teams player—he'd made the Pro Bowl in 2005 for his skills covering kickoffs and punts—and an auxiliary receiver. He caught 54 passes in his career, and four or more in a single game only eight times. In 2007, he caught four passes the entire regular season. In the three playoff games before the Super Bowl, he caught just one pass for four yards.

But as Super Bowl XLII began to creep closer, Tyree's role in the offense was becoming more and more important. The Giants did not know if star receiver Plaxico Burress would be able to play after suffering ankle and knee injuries. As the team practiced on Friday at the Arizona Cardinals' facility in Tempe, Arizona, Burress tried to test out his injuries by running routes. He couldn't. There was real concern that he might not be healthy enough to play in the biggest game of the year, and that Tyree and Sinorice Moss would have to pick up his reps.

If Tyree understood the magnitude of that responsibility on Friday, he did not rise to the occasion. While most Giants eyes were on Burress struggling to force himself through his injury, Tyree was dropping just about every pass thrown his way.

"Having a bad practice is dropping two balls," Tyree said. "I can't even count how many balls I dropped in that practice."

Tyree shook it off as best he could and approached Manning after the workout, partly to apologize for the lackluster performance and partly to let him know that his confidence was still high.

"And even before I could finish my sentence, he said, 'Don't worry about none of that. You know I'm coming at you.'"

Burress was able to play in the Super Bowl, and Sinorice Moss was inactive. Tyree was the fourth receiver. And Manning was true to his word. He threw five passes to Tyree in the game. The receiver caught two of the first four, including one for a 5-yard touchdown early in the fourth quarter that gave the Giants a 10–7 lead. Tyree hadn't caught a touchdown in over a year, and this one, to put his team ahead late in a game against an undefeated opponent in a Super Bowl, was undoubtedly the biggest reception of his career.

That honor would be short-lived.

Later in the fourth quarter, New England regained the lead when Tom Brady hit Randy Moss on a 6-yard pass, and it seemed as if Tyree and the Giants would become footnotes to the Patriots' perfect season. Two weeks earlier, when the Giants had advanced to the big game, Tom Coughlin began his meeting by challenging the players to name the team that had lost the Super Bowl two years ago. Hardly anyone could remember. That fate of anonymity was now two minutes and 42 seconds away for the Giants.

But the Giants still had something left in them. They started driving down the field. They converted a fourth-and-1 on a run by Brandon Jacobs behind fullback Madison Hedgecock. Manning threw a pass to Tyree and… it fell incomplete with 1:15 remaining.

It set up third-and-5 from the Giants' 44. The play came in, and Manning relayed it to the huddle: "62 Y Sail Union." Toomer and Burress lined up to the left, Tyree wide right with Steve Smith in the slot. The sail route is designed for

Smith to be the primary target near the sideline as Tyree runs a post pattern as a decoy to take the top off the coverage. The Giants had run the play about a dozen times during the year—it's a staple in their two-minute offense—and the ball had never gone to Tyree. This time, though, a Patriots defender stuck with Smith on the out route and freed up the middle part of the field for Tyree.

"We can win the game right now," Manning thought as he saw the defense react to Smith, knowing Tyree would be open.

Only the Patriots' defensive line had other ideas. They ran a stunt, and everything collapsed on Manning. Jarvis Green got a hand on Manning's shoulder. Richard Seymour had a grip on his jersey. But Manning's legs were still churning, and offensive linemen Richie Seubert and Shaun O'Hara, who were beaten on the stunt, kept blocking. Manning, at one point, saw a flash of white uniform in front of him and considered flipping the ball to that player. It was guard Chris Snee. Manning pulled the ball back on second though, and referee Mike Carey was about to call the play dead for a sack, when all of a sudden Manning escaped.

Tyree, meanwhile, had run his route and saw the chaos at the line of scrimmage. He started heading back toward the quarterback, as receivers are taught to do on scramble plays. This scramble seemed to be over, but Manning miraculously spun away from the glob of linemen, squared himself to the downfield, and did exactly what every quarterback since the dawn of the forward pass had been instructed not to do. He threw it blind down the middle of the field.

And there was Tyree, standing almost flat-footed and wide open, looking as if he were about to catch a punt. As the ball hung in the air, Patriots safety Rodney Harrison was en route, having abandoned his coverage on the left side of the field when he saw Tyree so open. The ball arrived. Harrison arrived.

"I went up with two hands, I felt it with two hands for a second, and I knew I lost control with one of my hands," Tyree said. "But I'm just thinking in my mind, 'I got it.'"

Harrison pulled at Tyree's right biceps as Tyree's right hand was pinning the ball against his helmet. The force from the safety was actually helping keep the ball in place, wedging it there so it wouldn't budge. Before Tyree and Harrison hit the ground, Tyree put his left hand back on the football and was gripping it just inches away from the grass. He and Harrison began wrestling for the ball, and Smith, the rookie receiver who was supposed to get the pass, ran over and pulled Harrison off Tyree.

"Get off him! Get off him!" Smith was yelling. "He caught it! He caught it!"

Harrison didn't know what Smith was talking about. In his mind, there was no way Tyree caught the pass.

Others were in equal disbelief. On the sideline, Tom Coughlin was yelling into his headset to coaches up in the press box: "Did he catch it? Did he catch it?" They kept telling him, "Yes! Yes!" but he kept asking anyway.

Manning, who had the presence of mind to call a timeout, ran to Tyree and asked him if he actually caught it. The quarterback knew that receivers always think they catch everything, so when Tyree first told him yes, Manning was skeptical.

"David, you're a Christian," Manning said. "Don't lie to me."

It was the last time in his career that Tyree could honestly say he caught the ball. He'd go on to spend parts of two more seasons in the NFL, get cut by the Giants, sign with the Ravens, but never again would he record a regular-season or postseason reception. He never even had another pass thrown in his direction.

Tyree's helmet from the catch is in the Pro Football Hall of Fame in Canton. The ball? It's in Plaxico Burress's living room in New Jersey.

"After he made the catch, we kept going," Burress said. "The referees didn't get the chance to switch the ball out."

Not until Manning hit Burress in the end zone for the game-winning touchdown at the end of the drive. It's the only football that can lay claim to having a place in two indelible moments of Giants history.

Tyree may not have the actual football, but his catch lives on. Every February, when the Super Bowl rolls around, clips of that pass being pinned to that helmet are shown on television. And there are other catches that have come along since then. Santonio Holmes dragging his toes in the end zone to win the Super Bowl for the Steelers a year after Tyree. Mario Manningham pulling in an over-the-shoulder catch along the sideline for the Giants against the Patriots in Super Bowl XLVI.

"Of all the catches that have come along since my catch, [Julian] Edelman's was, I feel personally, the only one that was comparable," Tyree said of the Patriots receiver's juggling grab in traffic in Super Bowl LI against the Falcons. "I'll give him that."

Comparable. But better?

"If I had to argue my case, there were factors that will very likely never be created again," Tyree said of his catch being the tops. The improbable player. The undefeated opponent. The scramble by the quarterback. "It's the dream scenario. That's what makes it what it was."

And makes it what it remains all these years later.

"No one has ever heard me say I made the greatest catch in Super Bowl history. I let other people do that," Tyree said. "But every time a great catch comes along, and this is my one claim to fame, they don't really compare it to anybody else's catch. They compare it to the helmet catch. Let's call that the standard. If it's not the best, it's certainly the standard."

NOBODY'S PERFECT

The game had just ended, bits of confetti were still fluttering in the air, and Giants coowner Steve Tisch had just become the first person ever to win both an Academy Award (he was producer for Best Picture winner *Forrest Gump*) and a Lombardi Trophy. As he climbed down the stairs from the stage set up in the middle of University of Phoenix Stadium in Arizona, where the Giants had come back and beaten the previously undefeated Patriots, 17–14, in Super Bowl XLII, one of the first questions asked of him was which meant more.

Tisch thought silently for about 10 seconds, then said he would give back his Oscar to win the Super Bowl.

Not surprising. He had just been holding the Lombardi for the first time in his life a moment earlier, so the emotional rush and attachment to it was much more immediate. But even years later, he stood by that hypothetical decision.

Why?

"Every great movie has characters, some you root for and some you root against," Tisch said. "There is excitement, there is action, there are surprises, there are situations that are unpredictable that the audience isn't ready for. Sometimes there is a surprise ending that you just can't believe happened. A good movie has great characters and a great script. A good movie takes 100 days to shoot with a crew of a couple hundred people.

"We had just seen in the Super Bowl a game that had every quality, all the excitement, all the surprises, all the action, all the people you root for, and all the characters you root against, played out live in 60 minutes on a football field. None of it was rehearsed, none of it was scripted. And that's why I would give back my

Academy Award. It was *real*. It was not scripted or rehearsed. It wasn't a movie. It was real life, in real time. And real exciting. A surprise ending."

One of the most surprising ever.

"That's why I love it," he said.

The Super Bowl ended with Patriots quarterback Tom Brady dejected and disappointed, but the week began with him amused. He even laughed a bit. Not at the audacity of an opposing player thinking his team might beat the Patriots in the Super Bowl, or any game for that matter. No, that was fine. That's what football players are supposed to believe. But when Giants wide receiver Plaxico Burress predicted a final score—and a low one—well, to Brady that was the strange part.

Burress had dropped his vision to a reporter from the *New York Post* named Brian Lewis, whose job was to watch the players walk by after their final practice in New Jersey and ask each of them if they had a prediction. It was a journalistic fishing expedition, and no one really expected any nibbles. There weren't any, either, until Burress walked past. When Lewis asked if he had a prediction, Burress simply gave him one.

"23–17."

Somewhat shocked, Lewis asked Burress to repeat it, just to make sure.

"23–17," he said.

He never used the "G" word, but it was about as close as anyone had come to guaranteeing a Super Bowl win since Joe Namath had with the Jets against the Colts. And this one seemed even more outlandish than that one.

This was a Patriots team that was not only 18–0, one win away from a perfect season, but also one that had set an NFL record by scoring 589 points. Brady's 50 touchdown passes set the record for most in a single season, and Randy Moss had caught 23 of them to set the receiving record. And just a month earlier, the Patriots had posted a 38–35 win over the Giants. Brady had already won three Super Bowl titles without ever losing in the big game.

Which is why the quarterback mocked chagrin when he arrived in Arizona and was told of Burress's prediction.

"We're only going to score 17 points?" Brady chuckled confidently. "OK. Is

Plax playing defense? I wish he had said 45–42 and gave us a little credit for scoring more points."

It turned out Burress gave the Patriots more credit than they would deserve.

The Giants defense in Super Bowl XLII managed to do what no team had been able to all season: slow down the Patriots. It was a simple game plan, really, that relied on using the front four players on the defensive line to put pressure on the quarterback—hit him, move him, make him uncomfortable—while the remaining seven players dropped into coverage and kept tabs on the receivers.

Simple to scheme, anyway. Executing it would be the key.

Which is why Osi Umenyiora, one of the Giants' top pass rushers, sat nervously at his table during a team breakfast the day of the game. Michael Strahan came into the room his usual bubbly self, cracking jokes and keeping everyone loose.

"He was doing his thing, talking, laughing loud," Umenyiora remembered. "And I remember telling him, 'Stray, listen, if we don't play our best game we're going to lose.'"

Strahan nodded and kept talking to others, the truth and intensity of Umenyiora's sober morning-of-the-game epiphany still not fully registered. So Osi tried again.

"I was like, 'No, no, no, listen to me, man,'" Umenyiora said, repeating his observation slowly with his eyes locked on Strahan's. "'This is the biggest game of our lives. If we don't play our best, we're going to lose and it's going to be our fault.'"

That got Strahan's attention.

"He brought everyone around him, said a few things, and then I could see it sink in," Umenyiora said. "I didn't hear him say another word until the actual game itself. It was crazy."

The defense had plenty of time to ruminate on the reality they faced, because the Giants received the ball to open the game and embarked on a 16-play, 63-yard drive that ate up the first 9:59 of the game. Despite the duration, it resulted only in a field goal and a 3–0 lead. Between the hoopla of the pregame ceremonies and the longevity of the first possession, by the time the Giants defense took the field, they had been standing around for close to an hour without playing a single snap.

The stagnation showed as the Patriots marched down the field for a touchdown on their first drive to take a 7–3 lead.

From there, though, the Giants' defense tightened up. They started to rattle Brady, whose mobility was hampered by an ankle injury he'd suffered in the AFC Championship Game. Four of the next six Patriots possessions ended in punts, one ended in a fumble, and another on a failed fourth-down attempt. The Giants, meanwhile, went ahead, 10–7, early in the fourth quarter when Eli Manning hit David Tyree for a touchdown.

It looked like the Giants might pull off the greatest upset in football history, but the Patriots were too good. They used a 12-play, 80-yard drive to eat up over five minutes of the fourth quarter and took a 14–10 lead with 2:42 remaining when Corey Webster slipped in coverage against Moss and Brady found him in the end zone for a touchdown.

The Giants, it seemed, had come up short. The Patriots were too good. Too prolific. Too… perfect.

"I was disappointed," Umenyiora said of his feelings as he and the defense came off the field having allowed the go-ahead score. "Obviously we had played so hard. They came back and they scored and we were disheartened."

There was only one thing the defenders could do. Hope.

So as the offensive linemen stood on the sideline waiting to take the field for a drive that would either result in the game-winning touchdown of a classic Super Bowl or an effort that would come up short, Michael Strahan marched back and forth in front of them.

"17–14 will be the final score," he told them. "Believe it and it will happen. 17–14, fellas. One touchdown and we'll be World Champions."

Strahan, it turned out, was channeling his father.

"The whole week leading up to the game, my dad kept telling me, 'You guys have already won this game, you just have to claim it. You won it, you just have to go through the formalities of playing,'" Strahan said. "Mentally, he was saying that you have to believe it. You have to accept it. You have to claim that you have this victory."

The captain started spreading that gospel.

"For me it was going over there to let them know basically what my dad had been telling me the whole week leading up to it," Strahan said. "I don't know if they believed it. Heck, sometimes I wonder if I believed it."

The Giants began the drive at their 17-yard line with 2:39 remaining. Manning hit Amani Toomer for a first down, but then the offense began to stall. On third-and-10 on the play after the two-minute warning, Manning hit Burress, but for only 9 yards. That left a do-or-die fourth-and-1.

The Giants handed the ball to Brandon Jacobs up the middle for a successful first down.

They were alive, but still 61 yards away from the end zone, and now with just 1:28 remaining. Manning scrambled for 5 yards on first down, threw an incompletion to Tyree on second down, and then, on third-and-5 from the Giants' 44, came "The Catch."

Manning eluded the Patriots' defense, was nearly sacked and pulled down by his jersey, kept his footing when he was flung, and threw a deep pass down the middle of the field that had no business being caught. Somehow, it stuck to Tyree's helmet, a play so astounding and memorable that it gets its own chapter in this book. A Miracle Moment within a Miracle Moment!

But the 32-yard completion would mean little without reaching the end zone. For that, the Giants had to go another 24 yards. And after Manning was sacked on the next play, they were out of timeouts with 51 seconds remaining.

Manning threw an incompletion and then, on third-and-11, hit rookie Steve Smith along the sideline for a gain of 12 to the 13. It's a play sandwiched between two of the most memorable catches in Giants history, but perhaps equally important.

Smith was pushed out of bounds to stop the clock, which allowed the Giants to settle themselves and call their play. As they broke the huddle, Manning grabbed Burress and told him: "If they go single, I'm throwing it."

Sure enough, the Patriots were in single coverage with Ellis Hobbs lined up against Burress. Plaxico's first thought was that he wouldn't be able to go to his left on the route because of the injured knee he was playing with the entire game, the one that had nearly scratched him from the lineup. But this was no time for doubt, and the thought was quickly dismissed.

"I said, 'Man, you know what, just run the route like you're healthy and if it goes, it goes,'" Burress said. "That's the conversation that I had with myself before the ball was hiked because I'm planting off the knee that's taped and I can't go left. I'm like, 'If you tear it up, it better be on the last play of the game.'"

The Patriots sent an all-out blitz, and Jacobs was in the backfield to help pick it up. That bought Manning enough time to turn to his left and loft the ball into the end zone for Burress.

"I see the ball up [in the air] and people in the stands," Burress said. "I turn 360 degrees running full speed with a bad knee. Then the feeling went out of me. I was, like, walking on air. I couldn't believe it just happened. I couldn't believe it was me of all people."

Touchdown. 17–14. Just like Strahan said it would be.

Plaxico Burress didn't know if his injured knee would allow him to make the game-winning catch in Super Bowl XLII, but he pushed through it and brought in Eli Manning's pass. (Streeter Lecka / Staff, courtesy of Getty Images)

"First of all, if we didn't do it, nobody would remember it," Strahan said of his speech. "But because we did everybody pays attention to it so I look like Nostradamus."

And it was almost just like Burress had predicted, too.

There were 35 harrowing seconds left. Enough time for the Patriots to attempt a few last-ditch efforts to get into field goal range and tie the score. Enough for them to score another touchdown to win it. Brady threw an incompletion and then was sacked by rookie Jay Alford, another huge play that often goes unrecognized. That set up third-and-20. On consecutive snaps, Brady threw long Hail Mary passes to Randy Moss, and the crowd of 71,000 at the University of Phoenix Stadium was breathlessly quiet while those footballs arced through the air. One glanced just off Moss's fingertips. Both fell incomplete, the final one with one second remaining in the game.

That allowed Manning and the offense to go back on the field and take a knee, a curtain call of sorts after their remarkable game-winning drive. The Patriots, it turned out, weren't so perfect after all.

It was, too, to be the final game of Strahan's Hall of Fame career.

"A good way to end it all," he said. "After that, for me, what else was there to do and what else was there to prove? It would have been nice to play the next year as a Super Bowl champion and travel to these cities and all that stuff and play other teams, but there is nothing like going out on top."

Not that it would have been easy to top this one.

"What a hell of a game," Strahan said. "Best football game I've ever been a part of."

SALSA TIME

"Get out of here!"

That was Victor Cruz's reaction when he came off a practice field in Indianapolis and was told that earlier in the day, while giving a press conference for her upcoming performance in the Super Bowl XLVI Halftime Show, none other than Madonna had broken into a salsa dance on stage in his honor.

Shock. Awe. Bewilderment.

That's when you know you've made it.

By the time Madonna was shimmying her hips and shuffling her feet, of course, Cruz had become an NFL sensation. His unique way of celebrating his touchdown receptions and honoring his Puerto Rican heritage had already become legendary. The Madonna homage put it over the top, made it mainstream. But it was just four months earlier that Cruz was a virtual unknown, a player who had blown his first opportunity to make an impression in a regular-season game, was awaiting his second, and knew that he would not get a third.

That first chance came in the 2011 opener against the Redskins when Cruz dropped what would have been a crucial first down in a loss. The Giants didn't want to stick around to see if an undrafted player from the University of Massachusetts would rebound and become a productive member of their team, so they signed veteran Brandon Stokley who was an experienced slot receiver. He helped them win their Week 2 game against the Rams but was injured in the process. The Giants had no choice but to turn back to Cruz as they faced the Eagles in Philadelphia in Week 3.

He started and wound up catching three passes for 110 yards with touchdowns

Victor Cruz emerged from nowhere and became one of the most beloved Giants of all time thanks to his timely catches and his posttouchdown salsa dancing. (Newsday LLC/ Jim McIsaac)

of 74 and 28 yards. But what really caught everyone's eye was what he did when he reached the end zone.

Mike Sullivan, the Giants' wide receivers coach, had been in Cruz's ear leading up to that September 25 game. It was Hispanic Heritage Month, and Sullivan wanted Cruz to do something special that would represent his culture and ethnicity, something to honor not only Puerto Ricans, but all Latin people.

"He was like, 'You gotta dance in the end zone!'" Cruz said.

Cruz said he would but later admitted it was just to get Sullivan out of his face.

"Low and behold, early in the game, I catch a pass and I'm going down the sideline and I'm about at the 5-yard line, and in my head I am like, 'Man, I gotta do this dance now,'" Cruz said. "I put the ball down and I just started dancing. I got really into it once I started doing it, and it kind of took a life of its own after that."

It was Cruz's grandmother who taught him the dance. In his autobiography, *Out of the Blue*, he wrote that she used dance instruction to focus his attention and energy when he was a rambunctious five-year-old bouncing off the walls of the family's apartment.

"We did it all—the merengue, the bachata, and the samba," he wrote. "My favorite dance of all, though, was the salsa. She'd put her favorite Tito Puente vinyl record on the record player, and we'd dance for hours in the kitchen. *Papi* would smile and laugh, sipping on his black coffee in his rocking chair."

After that first touchdown, breaking tackle attempts from Kurt Coleman and Nnamdi Asomugha, Cruz wrote in his book: "Without much second thought, I broke out the very same salsa dance my grandmother had taught me on East Twentieth Street twenty years before. Step, step, step. Move your arms. Shake your hips. The salsa!"

The Giants won the game, and afterward, when Cruz spoke with his mother, he was told that his grandmother loved the tribute. Not only that, but she now wanted him to do it after every touchdown he scored.

"It was kind of the first game for me," Cruz said of that day in Philadelphia. "Obviously I got a start, I got an opportunity, and I made the best of it. It's kind of where the Victor Cruz story originated."

It was actually a little over a year earlier that Victor Cruz was introduced to most of the sports-watching, NFL-following world. On August 16, 2010, he scored three second-half touchdowns in a preseason win over the Jets on national television. LeBron James tweeted about it, adding to the sensation. Rex Ryan, the coach of the Jets, told Tom Coughlin after the game: "I don't know who number 3 is, but holy shit!"

The headlines in the papers the following day were all about… Eli Manning. The Giants quarterback had been knocked out of the exhibition game early, taking a hit from linebacker Calvin Pace that jarred his helmet loose and caused a bloody gash on his forehead. Cruz was an after-deadline afterthought.

But it was a week before that game—August 11, to be exact—that Cruz first entered anyone's consciousness. It was a hot day in Albany at Giants training camp, and the team was suffering a spate of injuries at wide receiver. Steve Smith was unavailable. So too was Sinorice Moss. Coughlin was asked about the status of the group.

"Victor Cruz!" he shouted. "What do we need anybody for? We've got Victor Cruz!"

Then, after a beat and in response to a mix of polite giggles and blank stares from the audience, Coughlin added: "I'm serious."

Cruz had made a one-handed "catch" along the sideline in practice that morning (he landed out of bounds but held onto the ball) and had shown an ability to get open on some deep passes throughout camp, but there was no real indication yet that the undrafted rookie who wore the number 3 jersey would become one of the most popular players in team history. Only Coughlin's words.

"It feels good just to get in there and get some reps," Cruz said that day. "Some of the guys are hurt, so I'm just filling in and trying to get the plays down pat and play my role a little bit."

It turned out, all those years later, Cruz remembered that day, too. For all the passes he caught, all the accolades he achieved, even for the championship he helped win, Cruz said on the day he was released by the team in 2017 that his "favorite moment" as a Giant was catching Coughlin's eye on that day in Albany.

"Rookies don't impress Coach Coughlin very often," Cruz recalled. "To be able to turn Coach Coughlin's head and have him say something about me and really appreciate my talent level was a beautiful thing."

Cruz went from an obscure kid out of UMass and nearby Paterson, New Jersey, all the way to superstardom and a Super Bowl.

"Justice has been served," Coughlin said the night Cruz, the hustling rookie, caught those three preseason touchdowns against the Jets and cannonballed into New York's sports lore.

He made the team that year—the Giants couldn't very well cut him and try to get him on the practice squad without other teams gobbling him up, most notably the Jets, where Ryan had vowed to sign him if the Giants got rid of him—but was stashed on injured reserve with a hamstring injury a month into the season. The following season, 2011, he was back.

Despite the slow start, he wound up catching 82 passes for 1,536 yards and earned a Pro Bowl invite. He also caught nine touchdowns that season. Nine salsas.

And then, after going three postseason games without reaching the end zone, he caught a touchdown against the Patriots in the biggest game of the season.

Madonna never did do the salsa on the actual Super Bowl Sunday stage as part of her show.

But Victor Cruz did.

CURTAINS

The Giants and Jets have never met in a Super Bowl. That may be the only way that a clash between the two football teams who share a city and share a stadium could mean more than it did when they faced off on Christmas Eve, 2011. And even then, it might be up for debate.

That 2011 meeting was the most intense regular-season game many of the participants say they have ever played in. Its drama had been building since the offseason, when Jets coach Rex Ryan, fresh off two AFC Championship Game appearances, started talking about his squad taking over New York and becoming the "big brothers" in the rivalry. It simmered throughout the season, as both teams contended for the postseason and, by the time they reached this next-to-last game on their schedules, were each in need of wins to reach the playoffs.

But it all came to a head when the Giants walked into MetLife Stadium as the visiting team and were met with what they saw as the harshest slap in the face they had ever encountered.

On the walls outside the Giants' locker room are murals painted for each of the Super Bowl victories. At the time, there were three of them. But on that day, because the Jets were the home team, they did what their stadium protocol called for in a normal game.

They covered them up.

Long black curtains draped from aluminum poles that were hung on brackets in the cinderblock wall obscured those Super Bowl reminders.

First, a little geography from the bowels of MetLife Stadium. There are four full locker rooms off a concourse that runs in a ring around the playing field. In the southwest corner there are two, the Giants' home locker room and the one that is used by teams that visit to play the Jets. In the northwest corner is the Jets' home locker room and the one used by teams that visit the Giants. This is done to prevent teams who play each other from having adjacent locker rooms and from having to take the field through the same tunnel. So, for Jets home games, the visiting team uses the room next to the Giants' room. And when that happens, those Giants murals are covered. Most times, no one cares, because they're not Giants and are focused on playing the Jets anyway.

But in this case, well, it created quite a stir.

"It was a complete disrespect factor," said Giants offensive lineman David Diehl, still fired up by the slight: "It's their home game, but their side is on the complete other end. They don't walk through the same entrance, they don't go through the same way to walk past that. For us it was like, 'Yeah, this may be a split stadium, and yeah, you may be playing up against us, but if you are going to cover all that stuff up and show disrespect to the history of the Giants like it doesn't even matter, we're going to prove you wrong.' And not by saying it, but by our actions."

Kicker Lawrence Tynes had tried to pull the curtains away from the wall as he walked in to work that day, sliding them on the poles, but stadium workers just fixed them. Tynes gets a chuckle out of it now.

"It was kind of a big topic," he said of the pregame conversations in the locker room. "Players find stupid ways to be motivated, but there was kind of a little buzz in the locker room about it."

It was as if the Jets had insulted the mother of each Giants player personally. In the Jets' locker room, their players had no idea what was happening on the other side of the stadium. If any Giants weren't properly revved up for this game when they pulled into the parking lot, they were by the time they walked past those curtains.

"I don't understand why he did it," running back Brandon Jacobs said of Rex Ryan (who probably had no idea about the curtains, but whom the Giants blamed for the dis). "Don't cover our shit up. We took it personally. It pissed a lot of people off because they had no right to do that."

It did take a while for that anger to channel itself into football, because early in the

Victor Cruz and the Giants sailed past—and over—the Jets in a tense Christmas Eve Battle for New York. (Newsday LLC/ David Pokress)

game, it seemed as if the Jets were in control and they would be able to back up Ryan's bravado. They scored the game's first touchdown, and their defense was in control with a 7–3 lead late in the second quarter. The Giants' offense had trouble getting into gear, difficulty finding yards, and when the Jets downed a punt at the 1 with 2:37 left in the half, it seemed unlikely that the Giants would be able to find any more points before the break.

After two incompletions, on third-and-10 from the 1, the Giants were just looking to create some space to punt the ball back to the Jets. Eli Manning tossed a short swing pass to Victor Cruz on the right side. Cruz caught the ball at the 11, and the Giants thought to themselves: *Great! A first down!* But it turned out to be so much more.

Cruz turned it into a 99-yard touchdown, the longest play from scrimmage in Giants history, and one that is largely credited with igniting the run to the Super Bowl a little over a month later.

Two Jets, Antonio Cromartie and Kyle Wilson, converged on Cruz as he caught the pass, but he was able to split them to pick up more yardage. He maintained his balance and sprinted down the sideline. At around midfield, Jets safety Erik Smith dived trying to trip him up. Cruz high-stepped over him, then won a footrace to the end zone before spiking the football and breaking into a salsa on turf bearing the Jets' logo.

The Giants took a 10–7 lead and never again trailed in what eventually became a 29–14 victory.

"We definitely put them in a blender," Jacobs said. "They were embarrassed."

The win kept the Giants' playoff aspirations alive, but the Jets and Ryan never recovered. They would never again reach the postseason, and never be as close to it as they were in the first half of that game against the Giants.

"If you could point to a play that turned not just the game around, but maybe the season around, it was that play," Ryan said of Cruz's touchdown. "The Giants came out a totally different team, and they carried it through. It changed their fortune, and it certainly changed ours with that play and that loss… The fact that we never got into the playoffs since then, there's so much that changed after that."

The 99-yard touchdown is just one memorable moment in a game that had a number of them. The day was like an episode of *Seinfeld*, so full of classic stories that are remembered individually, but looking back it is difficult to fathom they were all packed into the same framework.

For some, it wasn't the Cruz touchdown that emphasized the Giants' dominance over the Jets that day, but the one after it, when Ahmad Bradshaw took a handoff from the 14 in the third quarter and obliterated safety Brodney Pool on his way to the end zone. Bradshaw lowered his shoulder, Pool went flying, and the running back was triumphantly holding the ball out before he even crossed the goal line.

For others, it was Giants running back D.J. Ware being tackled on his team's sideline and sliding into the legs of Tom Coughlin. The head coach jumped right back up and continued to coach the rest of the game despite having a hamstring injury so severe it pulled muscle from bone.

"I saw that and I was like, 'Holy shit! He's gonna die!'" Tynes said of Coughlin being upended. "And he just popped right up like he always does. Just tougher than woodpeckers' lips. He pops up and he's kind of hobbling around the rest of the game, but you know him, not a single complaint out of him the rest of the game."

And once the game was over, that's when the real fun began. Like after-credit scenes in a Marvel movie.

Former Giant and Super Bowl winner Plaxico Burress was with the Jets that season and played in the game against the Giants. Afterward, he was on the field catching up with some former teammates. One of them was Brandon Jacobs. As the two chatted and exchanged some holiday greetings, Rex Ryan walked past them.

Well, maybe not past them. More like he tried to walk through them.

"He bumped into me!" Jacobs recalled. "He bumped me pretty good. I remember Rex saying to wait until they won a Super Bowl, and I thought, *Your ass won't make it out of this game alive.* So, I turned around and I told him I'd kick his ass. He was messing with the wrong guy, and I'd punch him in the mouth. And he started talking and running his mouth."

Pretty soon the two men were jawing at each other on the field with photographers and players surrounding them, trading threats of physical violence and trying to get the last word. Jacobs never confirmed it, but those nearby say at one point he said to Ryan: "It's time to shut up, fat boy!"

"Did I plan on punching Rex Ryan? Absolutely not," Jacobs said. "But I just know his philosophy. I just know his philosophy and how he handles things."

That's because it was pretty much the same way Jacobs handled things. The two had more similarities than differences, which is probably why their personalities clashed on that postgame field.

But asked if he would have liked playing for Ryan, Jacobs was quick to answer.

"Oh absolutely. I can't deny that. I can't deny that at all. I'd be lying if I said no."

It would have come at a cost, though.

"I would have probably enjoyed playing for him, no question about it, but I don't think I would have become the overall guy that I am," Jacobs said. "The character of my being, none of that would have been the same. I'm not saying I would have been a bad person. There are plenty of guys who played for Rex Ryan who are great guys, great characters. But I think with the way I was, the way my attitude was set up, I think I needed a coach like Coach Coughlin to teach me not just about football but about being a man, about being a good father, stuff like that. I learned a lot of values from Coach Coughlin that help me even today. I got a lot more out of Coach Coughlin."

Jacobs admitted he was sometimes jealous of the Jets because of their relationship with their coach and the lax rules he employed.

"Those guys loved Rex," he said. "They loved playing for him. They loved talking about him. They'd do anything for him. Rex this, Rex that. We don't have to go in until this time, he doesn't care if we're late. Blah blah blah."

Of course, there was a downside to all of that.

"At the same time, though," Jacobs said, "you're getting your asses kicked every other week."

While Jacobs and Ryan were squaring off, there was still one unresolved issue: the curtains.

Diehl, Tynes, and long snapper Zak DeOssie ran through the tunnel to the Giants' locker room, but they did not stop there. They continued through that space out the door to the concourse, and, while still wearing their cleats and full uniforms and even with their hands taped up, they began yanking the black drapes down to the ground.

"We get in the locker room and immediately my first thought is *Let's go out there and pull these curtains back again*," Tynes said. "So, me and Dave Diehl and Zak went out there in our uniforms, pulling them back, saying, 'This is our house!' just kind of being stupid."

Diehl took it more seriously. He remains proud of the show he put on for reporters and cameras waiting outside the postgame locker room to go in and interview the players, only to have three of the most fired-up of them come out in the hallway and wreck the place.

"I wanted it to be known," he said. "You want to cover these things up? You wanted to do it before the game saying it was a distraction? Well, we just kicked your ass and now we're going to show that this is what the Giants' tradition and history is all about."

The Giants had held in much of their animosity toward the Jets during the week leading up to the critical game. Now it was all coming out.

"As Coach Coughlin always said: Modest in speech, superior in action," Diehl said. "That's something he always said to our football team. And they were the complete opposite. Not only from their team, but from their head coach. To hear that all season, to get yourself ready for that football game, that was one you had circled right when that schedule came out in the spring."

Diehl said the Giants made a huge statement that day.

"I definitely think we did," he said. "The feeling of us walking out there and ripping down those banners knowing that this is our stadium. You may say you are the big brother and you may put all of that stuff out into the press, but that doesn't make a difference in who is going to win or lose a game."

Close curtains.

"MAKE THEM GO TO MANNINGHAM"

If there was one thing Bill Belichick learned during his tenure as defensive coordinator of the Giants, it was how to eliminate an opponent's strength. Whether it was slowing down Jerry Rice or Jim Kelly or any of the other vaunted offensive players he faced in big games for Big Blue, he was usually able to pinpoint it and then take them out of the game.

It was a penchant he brought with him to the Patriots when he became their head coach. And it was a philosophy he used when he faced the Giants in Super Bowl XLVI on February 5, 2012, in Indianapolis. His Patriots led the Giants, 17–15, late in the fourth quarter, and as his defense prepared to take the field to try to make a championship-winning stop, Belichick gave them his orders.

"This is still a Cruz and Nicks game," Belichick said, reminding the Patriots defenders about the dangerous Victor Cruz and Hakeem Nicks. "I know we're right on them tight, but those are still the guys. Make them go to Manningham, make them go to Pascoe. Make sure we get Cruz and Nicks."

A few minutes later, Belichick got his wish.

So did the Giants.

With the Patriots locking up the top two receiving threats, Eli Manning was able to find Mario Manningham for a 38-yard completion down the New England sideline on the first snap from his own 12 that spurred the Giants to the game-winning touchdown eight plays later.

It wasn't the most incredible catch in Giants history. It wasn't the most flamboyant. It wasn't the most athletic or the luckiest or the most iconic.

But it was the most perfect execution of a pass and catch in a clutch situation that the franchise has ever had.

To many, it is remembered as Manning's finest throw of the thousands he had before and the thousands he had after. There was a window about the size of a bagel hole where the quarterback could put the ball safely into the hands of his receiver, avoiding the pair of defensive backs converging on the spot while keeping Manningham in bounds.

And Manningham? The player to whom Belichick wanted the Giants to throw the ball? He reached out and pulled the ball in over his shoulder, tapped both feet down in the field of play, and then skidded out of bounds... coming to a stop at Belichick's feet.

"I kind of turned into Space Jam with the stretchy arms," Manningham said. "It was great."

He knew, too, that he got both feet down. Even as the Patriots challenged the call, he was in the huddle with Manning and Nicks insisting he was in.

When he came to a stop, Manningham said he didn't remember hearing anything from the coaches and players on the Patriots sideline. It wasn't until a few days later, when NFL Films released the footage and audio it had captured from the game, that the receiver knew about Belichick's Manningham mandate.

"I understand," Manningham said. "Take away the hot guys. But it was the Super Bowl, and I was ready to play."

The door to this championship was similar to the one the Giants beat down to get to Super Bowl XLII, with one exception: they had a home game. The Giants hosted the Falcons in the NFC Wildcard Game on January 8, 2012—the first and so far only postseason home game ever played at MetLife Stadium—and trampled them, 24–2. Manning threw three touchdown passes, and the defense pitched a virtual shutout. The Giants stopped the Falcons on three fourth-down conversion attempts, including a pair of quarterback sneaks in the fourth quarter.

All that did was set the Giants up with the best team in the NFL. The Packers had gone 15–1 in 2011 and cruised to the top seed in the conference. It meant a return trip to Lambeau Field for a January playoff game, although this one was not as cold as the one four years earlier. Nor was it as close. The Giants used three touchdown passes by Eli Manning—including a 37-yard Hail Mary to Hakeem Nicks at the end of the first half—to earn a 37–20 victory. For the first time in a season in which they barely reached the playoffs, the Giants were thinking championship.

"I think we're a dangerous team," Coughlin said after the win in a rare public admission of optimism. But that's who these Giants were all of a sudden. They'd gone from a team that a month earlier needed to win two improbable games just to get into the playoffs to a team that was now two less improbable wins away from a title.

"I like where we are and how we're playing," Coughlin said.

Next stop: San Francisco for the NFC Championship Game. Manning had missed a practice that week with a stomach virus, showing some vulnerability to physical ailments for the first time in a career that had seen him play through serious shoulder and foot injuries to that point. But that belly bug was nothing compared to what awaited him in Candlestick Park.

He was pummeled into the soggy turf by the 49ers defense for most of the day, but each time, he got back up, scraped the clumps of mud and grass from his facemask, rolled his shoulders to get his pads back in their proper place, and went back to the line of scrimmage. Defenders hit him 20 times, six of them for sacks.

"We give him a lot of grief about his dorky appearance and he doesn't look like he has been in a weight room ever," defensive end Justin Tuck said. "But that guy is tough. He is like the Energizer Bunny. He keeps firing. He is the leader of this football team because of that."

While he threw for 316 yards and two touchdowns and completed 32 of 58 passes (the last two numbers establishing new Giants postseason records), it took more than Manning's grit to win the game. It took a special teams takeaway in overtime.

Rookie linebacker Jacquian Williams poked the ball away from punt returner Kyle Williams, and it was recovered by backup wide receiver Devin Thomas. That gave the Giants the ball at the 49ers' 24-yard line. The Giants would eventually get to the 6 before Manning centered the ball by taking a knee and Lawrence Tynes slogged his way onto the mucky field for a 31-yard field goal attempt. Four years earlier, Tynes had kicked a game-winning overtime field goal to send the Giants to the Super Bowl in frigid conditions on an icy surface. This time, he had to do it in a quagmire.

As the ball went through the uprights, holder Steve Weatherford ripped his own helmet off his head without even loosening the chinstrap and began sprinting around the field like a madman.

"We're going to the [blankety-blank] Super Bowl!" he screamed.

The Manningham catch in the Super Bowl two weeks later didn't get the Giants into the end zone. It only got them to midfield, and they still trailed by two points when Manningham's reception was confirmed by replay with 3:39 remaining. Manning continued to target Manningham on the drive; his next three passes went in that direction before his hit Nicks for 14 yards to reach the Patriots' 18 at the two-minute warning.

The Patriots wanted the Giants to throw the ball to Mario Manningham late in Super Bowl XLVI. The Giants obliged. (Al Bello / Staff, courtesy of Getty Images)

Now the Giants were in position to almost assuredly score the go-ahead points. It was just a matter of how—via touchdown or field goal?—and how much time they would leave for Tom Brady and the Patriots' offense to respond.

On the Giants' sideline, the long Manningham catch had sparked a flurry of activity from the special teamers. Weatherford, Tynes, and long snapper Zak DeOssie were preparing to win the Super Bowl.

"Steve and I always warm up for field-goal snaps near the side where we're about to kick," DeOssie said. "We are so excited-slash-nervous because we know our number is going to be called for this pending field goal to get the go-ahead points late in the Super Bowl. Nine times out of 10, you just bring your field-goal team out on the field, and we're going nuts over there. We're snapping. Steve's screaming. I'm screaming. We're screaming at each other. 'We're gonna do this! We're gonna win!'"

The trio was so sure of themselves that they were discussing who among them might be the MVP. Weatherford, who had the best game of his career on the biggest stage, boldly suggested that he might become the first punter to garner such honors. Tynes, who had already kicked two second-half field goals, said a third might give him the recognition.

"We're getting each other jacked up and there are more people crowding the sideline now because it's toward the end of the game and we're fighting for position to get our practice snaps in and getting more jacked up for a field goal than I ever have in my entire life. And then, all of a sudden . . ."

Touchdown.

Ahmad Bradshaw went up the middle on a 6-yard run to give the Giants a 21–17 lead with 57 seconds left. Actually, he ran about 5 ½ yards and then tried to stop before falling backward into the end zone for one of the most historic and ill-advised touchdowns in Super Bowl history. Instead of running out the clock and kicking the field goal with only a handful of seconds left, the Giants were giving the ball back to Brady with nearly a full minute left.

Just like the Patriots hoped they would.

"I just yelled: 'Don't score! Don't score!'" Manning said he told Bradshaw after the handoff. "Obviously, he heard me [because] he thought about it. I know it's tough for a running back. They see a big hole right there going for a touchdown. I think something almost had to pop into his head like something was up, this is a little bit too good to be true… I think he didn't quite know what to do. He said, 'Hey, I have a touchdown, I'm going to take it.'"

"It's a tough feeling," Bradshaw said of the uncommon urge to not score. "I didn't think about it and then Eli says, 'Don't score! Don't score!' as soon as he gives me the ball. It didn't click until like the 1-yard line. I tried to go down and tap down, but the momentum took me in."

The Giants attempted a two-point conversion after the Bradshaw touchdown, but failed, and led 21–17. When Tuck sacked Brady on third down, it looked like a game-sealing play for the Giants, but the Patriots converted on fourth-and-16 with 32 seconds left to remain alive. They stayed that way up until the final snap of the ball with five seconds left, when Brady threw the ball into the end zone from his own 42.

The pass was intended for tight end Aaron Hernandez, but safety Kenny Phillips managed to swat it away. Even that didn't win the game for the Giants, though. The ball fluttered, and Rob Gronkowski dived in an attempt to snare it before it hit the turf.

He could not.

"The first [Super Bowl] was kind of a blur," DeOssie said. "It was my rookie year, and my head was spinning. I joked with some of my fellow draft picks at the time, at the second one, we joked about paying attention this go-around. I just sort of took time to appreciate the opportunity to be there from start to finish and I remember a lot more."

Many other players and coaches say any time they walk around Lucas Oil Stadium to this day, if they look closely enough, they find pieces of silver or blue confetti from that game lodged in cracks or stuck to the turf. Is it really from the Giants' celebration? Maybe. But there is a bucket in the rafters of the stadium, just above the 35-yard line, that can be seen from the field. When the Giants won and the confetti was triggered, that one bucket failed to tip its load into the air. So it remains there, full of tiny slivers of paper and Mylar. Waiting, perhaps, for the next Giants championship.

Giants fans cherish that game, as well. Maybe because there was so much to remember. Like Chase Blackburn's interception covering Gronkowski far down the field; Blackburn had been out of football and working as a substitute teacher when the Giants called him in November and signed him to become their starting middle linebacker. There was Victor Cruz's touchdown and obligatory salsa dance.

There was a pass from Brady to a wide-open Wes Welker in the fourth quarter that would have all but sealed the victory for the Patriots with a first down, but the normally sure-handed receiver dropped it.

And, of course, Manningham's catch that sparked the comeback.

At Belichick's request.

CATCHING SUPERSTARDOM

It was the kind of moment most players spend their whole careers, maybe even their whole lives, in search of. The play that doesn't just define them, but becomes bigger than they. Franco Harris had one with his Immaculate Reception. David Tyree certainly had one on the biggest stage of all, the Super Bowl. Others, too, were able to rise to the occasion and stamp their likeness on the collective memory of the football world.

What could possibly be better than that?

Don't ask Odell Beckham Jr. He might tell you.

Beckham had such a moment, and it transformed him. In some ways, it took him over. He was one person for the first 22 years and 18 days of his life leading up to November 23, 2014, when he took the field as a promising rookie wide receiver for the Giants in a prime-time game against the Cowboys. He has been forced to become someone else ever since.

Which is why, even though making that play that night at MetLife Stadium brought Beckham everything he thought he ever wanted from football—fame, fortune, respect, attention, gravitas, influence, marketability, and a legacy—he looks back on it and seems to wonder if it was worth it.

What if the pass had glanced off his hand? What if he hadn't caught it with just three fingers, yanking it in toward his body as he fell backward into the end zone? It was one catch. Would anyone have noticed it missing from the collection once his stats were assembled? He still would have set all kinds of rookie records for receptions and yardage. He still would have been named NFL Offensive Rookie of the Year. He still would have gone to all the Pro Bowls. The Giants still would have lost that game. And he probably still would have been inundated with commercial opportunities and become the rare football player whose stardom transcends the sport.

But he would have been able to be the same person he was before the catch. He wouldn't have to live up to the catch, be overshadowed by it. Consumed by it.

Which is why, when he looks back on that grab that made him the Odell we think of these days, that caught the attention of the NFL and the entire sports world, he has one word to describe it.

"Bittersweet," he said.

What an odd choice of words for something that should be celebrated and ought to be enjoyed. So why bittersweet?

"Because I think my career is much more than one catch," he said. "It's funny when people are like, 'Oh, it's only this one-handed catch and blah blah blah.' Yet, anytime a catch happens, I'm compared to it. So, it was a moment that obviously changed my life forever. For better or worse."

It was the first play of the second quarter, the Giants were up 7–3 over the Cowboys, and the viewing audience was just coming back from a commercial break. That's when Manning dropped back, rolled a little to his right, and flung the ball 50 yards down the field for his rookie wide receiver. Dallas cornerback Brandon Carr tugged at Beckham's jersey, and flags flew in to signal the pass interference call that was going to bring the Giants to the doorstep of the end zone.

But then something amazing happened. Beckham, thrown off balance by the defensive penalty, falling backward into the end zone, reached up with his right hand and plucked the ball out of the air. He tumbled over on the ground, got to his feet, tossed the ball away, and extended his arms. It was, for just about everyone in the stadium that night, the greatest catch they had ever witnessed.

And the crowd went… silent.

There was an eerie moment of collective blinking and what-did-I-just see? head-shaking before anyone seemed to realize that Beckham actually made the catch. It was *Matrix*-meets-Madden, part video game and part movie, and it felt like there had been a ripple in the time-space-football continuum.

Even the announcers on the NBC broadcast, the normally unflappable Al Michaels and Cris Collinsworth, were stunned.

The man who found the perfect words to describe the Miracle on Ice when the United States hockey team beat the Soviet Union in 1980 was rendered nearly speechless by Beckham's catch.

"There's a flag, Beckham a one-handed catch," Michaels said, barely raising his voice. "How in the world…?"

The high-def replays and close-ups of the catch each made it more spectacular. Eventually the footage got so close that it became clear Beckham did not catch the football with one hand, but with two fingers and a thumb, pinching it between his digits and maintaining control of it as he hit the turf.

"That is absolutely impossible what he just did," Collinsworth said. "That may be the greatest catch I've ever seen in my life."

Added Michaels: "There's your play of the year and maybe, I don't know, the decade. That's just incredible."

Giants guard Geoff Schwartz was the first teammate to reach Beckham in the end zone after the touchdown, but he said his two memories of that play came just before and just after the catch.

"I was blocking [Cowboys defensive lineman] Henry Melton and Eli was doing a half-roll, which tells the defender that the ball is going deep. And Henry Melton yells out, 'Oh, shit!' because he knew Eli was going to throw the ball. Obviously, he doesn't know what is happening behind him, but he knows Eli had a clean pocket and was throwing the ball deep. It was funny that he said that. He knew something was coming."

Then, after the touchdown, Schwartz remembers walking from the end zone to the Giants' sideline. He was just back from an injury and was not on the extra-point team, and as he made the journey back to the bench, the excitement around him was palpable and eerily audible.

It wasn't loud cheering like when a team wins a championship. It was more confusion about what those fans had just seen, their making sure it was real.

It was the sound of awe.

"It was unlike anything I've ever really experienced before or since," Schwartz said of the vibrations. "As more people kept seeing the replay, I remember a buzz.

There was an actual, physical buzz in the stadium as people looked at the play on the jumbotron… I didn't realize the moment quite yet, but I remember the buzz."

The whirlwind wasted no time picking Beckham up and tossing him about. LeBron James tweeted about the catch after watching it on the NBC broadcast, and before long, the two were buddies hanging out in the offseason and rooting each other on. Beckham's jersey from the game against the Cowboys was shipped off and displayed at the Pro Football Hall of Fame. Two days after the catch, he was in a mall on Long Island signing photographs of the grab by the hundreds, the only thing slowing his handwriting down being the color printer at Steiner Sports that was spitting out the images. It might as well have been churning out hundred-dollar bills the way the public was gobbling up anything and everything that had to do with the miracle catch.

With all the attention came jealousy. Beckham morphed into a target. The good vibes and euphoria from the catch lasted about a month before his newfound fame bubbled over into notoriety.

On December 21, 2014, Beckham was unhappy with the way the Rams were treating him. They were serving up some extra hits, some late shoves, and eventually Beckham had enough. After he was tackled by linebacker Alec Ogletree a few yards into the Giants' bench area, he came up chirping, and Ogletree pushed him back to the ground. That set off a brawl between the teams that led to several ejections, although Beckham stayed in the game.

Almost exactly a year later, on December 20, 2015, the Giants faced the Panthers at MetLife Stadium. Beckham was involved in a pregame argument with several opposing players—including cornerback Josh Norman and practice squad player Marcus Bell, who was wielding a bat—and that confrontation spilled over into the actual game.

Beckham became frustrated by Norman's physical play (as well as his own dropped pass on the opening snap of the game that would have been a touchdown). Beckham was flagged for three unsportsmanlike conduct penalties in the game, including one for launching himself helmet-first at Norman. That led to a one-game suspension.

Odell Beckham Jr. was one of the most dynamic players to ever wear a Giants uniform. His one-handed catches and touchdowns thrilled Giants fans from 2014 until he was traded to the Browns in 2019. (Newsday LLC/Jim McIsaac)

"I hope I pulled back the mask on who this guy really is," Norman said after the game. "He's got the maturity of a little kid."

Controversy found Beckham off the field, as well. Viral videos of his antics spread around the Internet faster that the highlights from his games. Prior to the Giants' playoff game at the end of the 2016 season, he and other Giants receivers went to Miami on their day off and partied on a yacht with rapper Trey Songz, posting photos and videos of their adventure as they went along. The Giants tried to dismiss the antics, which would have been much easier to do if they had won the game against the Packers less than a week later. Instead, Beckham dropped several passes, and the Giants were knocked out of the postseason. Then, there was another controversy. A hole was punched in the wall outside the Giants' locker room at Lambeau Field just as Beckham was passing by. No one ever saw him put his fist through the drywall, and he has never copped to the act, but it was another black eye for Beckham's public profile, and it caused General Manager Jerry Reese to insist that the mercurial wide receiver "grow up."

The following year, Beckham fractured his ankle in Week 6 after initially injuring it in the preseason. A young safety for the Browns was trying to make a name for himself by bringing down the big dog, and he took what many felt was a cheap low shot at Beckham that sent him limping off the field. Beckham returned to action in Week 2 of the season but was clearly not playing at full strength. Eventually, the weakened ankle was snapped in the game against the Chargers and Beckham's season was over.

He wanted to be known for more than just the one-handed catch. Now he was, but for the wrong reasons.

Despite all the distractions, Beckham is undisputedly a phenomenally talented football player and wide receiver. And the name Odell has become to one-handed catches what Xerox is to photocopies. Their brand names have become synonymous with their product. Just like Xerox, Beckham has pretty much given up fighting the fight over trademarks and copyrights.

So it is that just about anytime a football player makes a catch with one hand, be it in high school, college, or the NFL, Beckham's name is conjured. Heck, anytime anyone catches anything with one hand—a beer tossed by a buddy from the fridge, an orange in the produce section of the grocery, a rolled-up pair of socks at the laundromat—there is a good chance Beckham's name will be uttered.

Inevitably, many of those Odell wannabes find their way to one destination: his phone. Hardly a day has passed since 2014 that he has not been tagged, alerted, direct-messaged, or in some other social media way made aware of someone else's one-handed catch of something caught on video and posted online. Not even being traded from the Giants to the Browns on March 13, 2019, could stop that stream. That's something that he will have to continue to deal with for the rest of his career, possibly the rest of his life.

That's what makes it so hard. He's perpetually the 22-year-old kid reaching high over his head for a wobbly football in so many people's minds. But in his own, he's grown beyond it. At least he's tried to.

"It was just a very iconic moment," he said. "It was just a very prolific moment in my career, so I don't mind getting tagged on Instagram seeing a bunch of nice catches.

"It kind of gives me motivation to do something crazier."

RESOURCES

Newsday
The *New York Times*
The *New York Post*
Sports Illustrated
ESPN
NFL Films
Giants.com
NFL Game Statistics & Information System
ProFootballReference.com

Parcells: Autobiography of the Biggest Giant of Them All by Bill Parcells
A Team to Believe In by Tom Coughlin
L.T.: Over the Edge by Lawrence Taylor
Out of the Blue by Victor Cruz
Giants: 70 Years of Championship Football by John Steinbreder
Guts and Genius by Bob Glauber
Eli Manning: The Making of a Quarterback by Ralph Vacchiano
Lombardi and Landry by Ernie Palladino
Belichick by Ian O'Connor
The Football Encyclopedia: The Complete History of Professional Football by David S. Neft, Richard M. Cohen, and Rick Korch

ACKNOWLEDGMENTS

Football people aren't always known for their ability to open up. So thank you, first of all, to the players, coaches, and executives who are quoted in this book and who were so very generous with their time and their memories. This book was as much about their exploits as it was about how they felt and what they were thinking while achieving such greatness, and they were able to recall details with amazing precision and a fascinating sense of narrative. There were very few doors I knocked on while reporting this book that were not flung wide open for me, and I'll always appreciate that. I hope I told your stories to the readers with the same passion and nuance and reverence as you told them to me.

Thanks to everyone behind the scenes at the Giants, too, without whose help I would not have been able to get to all of those doors and connect. Pat Hanlon, Jen Conley, and Doug Murphy went above and beyond to try to get me whatever I needed, whether it was an old photograph or an up-to-date cell phone number. Hanlon was surprisingly patient and cordial about it, too, which may have been the biggest Miracle Moment of the process from my perspective!

I write just about every day for *Newsday*, but writing a book like this was an entirely new experience. So thank you to Julie Ganz at Skyhorse Publishing, who was there to answer all of my silly questions, help me with the pacing of the project, and serve as a veteran presence to this rookie. We worked together on this through the 2018 season, and Julie, a Giants fan, was always on the lookout for one more up-to-date Miracle Moment to spring forth from that campaign. Sadly, the Giants finished 5–11. Maybe this year, Julie. There's always the second edition.

Thanks to everyone at *Newsday* who has encouraged and inspired me throughout my nearly quarter of a century (yikes!) working there. Sports Editor Hank Winnicki and Deputy Sports Editor Mike Rose make it easy for me to do my job, and there are plenty of copy editors on the desk there in Melville who make me seem like a much better writer and reporter than I am. Thanks, too, to *Newsday*'s Research Manager Laura Mann, who was so helpful when it came time to comb through the archives for old photos that would be perfect fits for this book.

There are many colleagues and competitors with whom I work on a regular basis, and I think they'd be surprised to know how helpful they have been in this process… especially since most of them didn't even know about it! The pregame conversations with Vinny DiTrani, Paul Schwartz, Bob Glauber, and Neil Best were so rich with information and background about the events I wrote about here but did not witness firsthand. Thanks to Steve Serby, Judy Battista, Kim Jones, Hank Gola, Ralph Vacchiano, Art Stapleton, and Mark Cannizzaro for being unsuspecting sounding boards and resources, as well. And thanks to the late Ernie Palladino, who I know would have enjoyed this book and showered me with embarrassing shouts of "Author! Author!" for many years to come.

Two writers I met very early in my career have been influential and helpful throughout. Authors Dan Paisner and Tom Clavin have always been there for me, nudging me along and setting shining examples of the kind of work I hope to create. It was Dan who suggested an idea for a book and Tom who put me in touch with Skyhorse to try to sell that idea. That project never took off, but it led to this book. An audible! So, thank you.

Finally, thank you to my wife, Amanda, and our children, Charlie, Abby, and Spencer. Your patience and support, not only during my work on this book, but in everything and always, can never be repaid. Whether it is a missed lacrosse game, a family dinner interrupted by a phone call, or a temper tantrum I throw in frustration, your understanding in the face of the many disruptions I bring into our home overwhelms me even as I know I should have exhausted it long ago. I love you guys, and I could not have done this—or anything else, for that matter—without you.

ABOUT THE AUTHOR

Tom Rock is an award-winning sports journalist for *Newsday* in New York, where he has worked since 1996. He has covered the NFL since 2006 and the New York Giants since 2008. His articles have been cited in the 2005 edition of *The Best American Sports Writing* and recognized by the APSE (Associated Press Sports Editors), New York Press Club, Press Club of Long Island, and the New York City Chapter of the Society of Professional Journalists. He is the author of the novel *Game Seven.*

He lives in Sound Beach, New York, with his wife, Amanda, and their three children.